Is there Poverty In Your Cup of COFFEE?

A PROFILE OF THE GLOBAL COFFEE VALUE CHAIN

FRED KAWUMA

Foreword by Dr. Vanusia Nogueira
Executive Director of the International Coffee Organization (ICO)

Dedication

To the farmers globally who labour and toil — many under extreme poverty — to produce the coffee that is so loved, the drinkers who pay for it, and the value chain players who ensure that the final consumers get coffee's pleasure in all its forms.

Acknowledgements

I am extremely grateful to all the individuals who contributed to the information in this book and the different resources that I consulted. Several people helped with content validation, and their contribution is greatly appreciated. David Sseppuuya's invaluable advice regarding the content and layout, as well as editing the manuscript, made a significant contribution to this book's completion and the form it took. The support from my dear wife Miriam and our children made all the difference throughout this journey, and I am very grateful to them. I thank everyone who made this journey a success, and I have said more about this in Chapter Twelve.

info@fredkawuma.com

Second Printing

ISBN 978-9913-9743-0-1

P.O. Box 10974, Kampala, Uganda. Tel: +256 776 700190
Email: info@fredkawuma.com
Website: www.fredkawuma.com

X (formerly Twitter): @fkawuma
LinkedIn: fkawuma

Contents

Foreword

This book is a call for reflection.

Instead of telling you what I think before you delve into its contents, I would like you to reflect on the simple pleasure of enjoying a cup of coffee and to consider the people and processes behind it. It might be a can of cold brew by the beach or a steaming cup of coffee in the wintertime, perhaps mixed with milk or savoured in its pure form. Another option, if you are curious, is to flip through the pages and discover how coffee is made in certain African and

Middle Eastern countries. Rest assured - the flavours are equally delicious.

The choice between poverty and prosperity is yours to make.

I urge you to make time to read this book. It unveils the history of coffee consumption, tracing its global spread, and explores how coffee production got to where it is today. And, if you're not already aware, it also sheds light on the many health benefits associated with our beloved beverage.

Regrettably, however, global statistics indicate significant poverty in coffee-producing countries. Is this poverty a coincidence, a cause, or a consequence of coffee production? In truth, it is a complex issue with no singular solution. What is clear is that many producing families and countries require support in health, education, and infrastructure to achieve a decent quality of life and prosperity. This assistance is crucial in order for them to progress and maintain the beautiful and essential environments where coffee is cultivated.

So, why not set off on a coffee tour of the world? Read on and be our guest. And if you have any fresh ideas to contribute to Chapter 9, I am sure the author will appreciate them.

I hope you enjoy this book as much as I did. Please savour every moment!

Dr Vanusia Maria Carneiro Nogueira
Executive Director, International Coffee Organization (ICO)
London, United Kingdom

Endorsements

This is a well-researched work presenting a global view of the coffee value chain. The author articulates the Ethiopian coffee culture very well, and humanity needs to appreciate coffee as Africa's gift to the world. Most importantly, all efforts should be made to address the issue of poverty among coffee producers. Evidently, his decades of experience in the sector come through in this book. I congratulate Dr Frederick Kawuma on this significant milestone and endorse his book without reservation.

H.E. Hailemariam Desalegn
Former Prime Minister, Federal Democratic Republic of Ethiopia

I congratulate Dr Fred Kawuma on writing this masterpiece on coffee. It is an authoritative overview of the global coffee value chain, with a pointed focus on addressing the issue of poverty among coffee producers.

Dr Kawuma's book provides important information for understanding coffee consumption in different markets, including insights on coffee and health, coffee and culture, and the different uses of coffee. The book reflects on the challenges of achieving prosperity for coffee producers to enable them to live dignified lives, and suggests the possibilities of partnerships to enhance their livelihoods.

The author is an effective ambassador for African coffee, whose work has catapulted him to become a global coffee ambassador championing the cause of coffee producers worldwide. The book is written in an easy-to-read style and provides important insights into understanding the workings of the global coffee value chain.

It is a must-read, and I recommend it to coffee lovers, enthusiasts and the general public.

Rt. Hon. Dr Ruhakana Rugunda
Former Prime Minister
Republic of Uganda

An excellent multidimensional description of the global coffee business, Fred Kawuma's book does not avoid the critical issue that the majority of coffee growers around the world do not earn a sustainable and living income. Find out why, as you read the book! Many of the reasons are spelled out, as well as a description of initiatives to address the producers' plight, like that of the Global Coffee Platform, whose current ambitious goal is to close the living income gap by 25% for one million small-holder coffee growers by 2030. But much more is needed. Fred's practical calculation of growers' income loss in the last 43 years is staggering!

I urge you to read this unique book while asking yourself what can be done to help coffee growers make more money. Not simple but badly needed if we, coffee lovers, want to retain the diversity of supply we have today. The book describes this well. Yes, Fred, we have to bless those who produce coffee... and do much more. Great book!

Dr Carlos Henrique Jorge Brando
Director, P&A Marketing, Brazil
Chairman of the Global Coffee Platform (GCP)

Is There Poverty in Your Cup of Coffee? is a captivating book that eloquently captures insightful information of the entire global coffee industry. This book is an enjoyable and informative read and takes us on a journey to describe who the producers and consumers are, the attributes of the beverage, innovations, cultures, and emerging issues the industry faces. Fred's passion and contributions to the global coffee industry are inspiring. He has had a distinguished career as a coffee professional and has been involved in many initiatives that have shaped the coffee journey at the national, regional and international levels. I wholeheartedly endorse this book and encourage every coffee lover to read it.

Ambassador Solomon S. Rutega
Secretary-General
Inter-African Coffee Organisation (IACO)

A captivating overview of the global coffee value chain, as narrated by the African Coffee Ambassador, Dr Fred Kawuma. Most importantly, the concern of poverty among coffee producers has been well articulated, as well as possible strategies to mitigate this. I wholeheartedly endorse this book.

Madhu Bophanna
Trustee, India Coffee Trust

Preface

Hello, welcome to Fred's Coffee Shop.

Please sit down. Fred will be with us in a few minutes to talk about coffee.

I know Fred wants to talk about poverty, and that typically means talking about money. But if poverty is only about money, I would merely ask you how much money you make and how much you have saved. That does not seem to be a very welcoming way to invite you to Fred's.

I want to welcome you, all of you, to this important conversation. So how can I welcome you? What is your name? Do you have a family? Do tell me about your family members? What education do you have? Is your health good and do you have good health care? What do you do for a living? Do you feel safe from violence or crime? Where do you live? How is the local water supply and are you on the sewer mains? Are you making ends meet? I want to understand your situation before I react. I want to get to know you. Can I order you a cup of coffee? Can I recommend Colombian coffee today? It's particularly good. How do you like your coffee?

Let me introduce myself. I am Jamie Coats, CEO of a company, Wise Responder Inc, which was set up by Oxford University to bring the science of measuring multidimensional poverty to commercial sectors and investors. The Oxford Poverty and Human Development Initiative (OPHI) has pioneered the ability to measure poverty by mathematically scoring the actual living circumstance of households in areas like education, health, living standards, employment, and safety. Now over forty governments have official national multidimensional poverty measures to supplement their official monetary measures. I call this seeing with two eyes, with one eye seeing people by their human circumstance and with the other eye seeing people's financial situation.

Ah, here is your Colombia cup of coffee. Smells wonderful. Let us discuss its origins. With the help of friends at the Federación Nacional de Cafeteros, Colombia, especially Jose Leibovich, it is now possible to tell you that the percentage of coffee households who are multidimensionally poor by official Colombia government measures. The answer is that 32.8% (584,191) of people in Colombian coffee households are poor. The main deprivations are 1) Low educational achievement, 2) Informal employment, 3) Lack of access to improved water sources, 4) Inadequate sanitation, 5) Inadequate floor materials, and 6) Illiteracy. One-third of the coffee in this cup was produced by people living in acute poverty. It is quite a conversation that we need to have where we think about how much we pay for coffee and how to improve the circumstances in which coffee producers toil and live to deliver this wonderful beverage.

I want to thank Juan Esteban Orduz of the World Coffee Producers Forum for working with CAF - the Latin American Development Bank - to invite Wise Responder to work with Professor

Jeffrey Sachs of Columbia University on the development of a guide to create National Coffee Sustainability Plans. These include both monetary and multidimensional poverty measurement, which led me to meet Fred.

I commend the conversation that Fred is inviting you to have here. Fred wants us to ensure that coffee farmers are paid fairly and live in decent circumstances. He wants your cup of coffee to taste even better and for it to leave you with a satisfied smile derived from knowing that your purchase creates a better world. But as Fred will relate, the plight of coffee producers is not necessarily improving and, in many cases, it is worsening. I was buying a cup of coffee at the Bodleian Cafe at Weston library in Oxford and was impressed that there was a sign saying the coffee was organic, environmentally friendly, and fair trade. I asked the barista, "Do you know what proportion of poverty there is in the coffee you brew?" He replied, "I don't know, they don't tell us."

It is now possible to tell everyone what poverty is in a cup of coffee. There is no broad will yet to do the measuring or to share the results. So, Fred is asking you to imagine that in coffee shops worldwide the conversation starts to demand that we be told what the poverty is in our cup of coffee and, in turn, we ask what is being done to reduce the poverty for coffee producers.

Please listen to Fred through the words of this book and join the conversation. Please add your voice to the call to reduce to zero the poverty in your cup of coffee.

Jamie Coats
CEO Wise Responder, Inc.

Glossary

Arabica coffee: One of the two primary species used in commercial coffee production. Arabica coffee (Coffea arabica) is highly regarded for its superior quality, and accounts for a significant portion of the world's production.

Barista: A skilled professional trained in preparing and serving various coffee-based beverages. They work in coffee shops, cafes, and restaurants.

Brewing: The process of extracting flavours, aromas, and compounds from coffee grounds to create a beverage. Popular methods include pour-over, French press, Espresso, Aeropress, cold brew, and drip coffee maker.

Café: A casual dining establishment that typically serves coffee, tea, light meals, pastries, and desserts.

Cappuccino: A popular espresso-based coffee beverage that consists of three main ingredients: espresso, steamed milk, and milk foam.

Connoisseurs: Experts with a deep understanding, knowledge, and appreciation for art, food, wine, or coffee. Coffee connoisseurs possess a sophisticated understanding of different coffee beans, roasting techniques, brewing methods, and the nuances of flavour profiles.

Cup-tasting: Often referred to as cupping, it is a method used to evaluate and assess the aroma, flavor, acidity, body, and overall quality of coffee.

Espresso: A concentrated beverage brewed by forcing hot water through finely-ground coffee beans, made using an espresso machine, which pressurises water at high temperatures, passing it through the coffee grounds quickly.

Frappuccino: A blended ice beverage made popular by Starbucks. It is a trademarked name for a specific type of frozen coffee drink. It typically consists of a blend of ice, milk, flavoured syrups, and coffee, all blended to create a smooth and icy texture. Variations include different flavours like mocha, caramel, vanilla, and seasonal offerings.

Latte: A popular coffee drink made with espresso and steamed milk, topped with a small amount of milk foam. It is a creamy and milder beverage compared to some other espresso-based drinks.

Macchiato: An espresso-based coffee beverage typically consisting of a shot of "stained" or "marked" with a small amount of milk or milk foam. "Macchiato" in Italian means "stained" or "spotted."

Mocha Coffee: Combines espresso with steamed milk and chocolate. Can be topped with whipped cream and sometimes chocolate shavings.

Mocha Pot: Stovetop coffee maker that brews coffee by passing boiling water pressurised by steam through ground. Also known as a "stovetop espresso maker" or an "espresso pot.".

Palate: The range and sensitivity of flavours that an individual can perceive and distinguish while tasting coffee. It involves the ability to identify various taste components such as sweetness, acidity, bitterness, and specific flavour notes.

Robusta coffee: *(Coffea canephora)* is the other primary species of coffee plant cultivated for commercial production alongside Arabica, comprising about 40% of global production. Robusta beans are known for their robust flavour, higher caffeine content, and resilience in different growing conditions compared to Arabica beans.

Terroir: A French term that encompasses the environmental factors that influence and impart unique characteristics to agricultural products and, in the context of this book, refers to coffee. The concept suggests that the specific geographic location, soil composition, climate, topography, and other environmental factors can significantly impact coffee's final taste, aroma, and overall quality.

Abbreviations

ABICS	Associação Brasileira da Indústria de Café Solúvel (Brazilian Association of Soluble Coffee Industry)
AfCFTA	African Continental Free Trade Area
AFCA	African Fine Coffees Association
AJCA	All Japan Coffee Association
ASCA	Australian Specialty Coffee Association
AU	African Union
CCAB	China Coffee Association Beijing
CICC	Cocoa and Coffee Inter-professional Council of Cameroon
CQI	Coffee Quality Institute
DNA	Deoxyribonucleic acid
DRC	Democratic Republic of Congo
EU	European Union
ECF	European Coffee Federation

FAQ	Fairly Average Quality
FNC	Federación Nacional de Cafeteros de Colombia (National Federation of Coffee Growers of Colombia)
GCP	Global Coffee Platform
GBE	Green Bean Equivalent
ICA	International Coffee Agreement
ICC	International Coffee Council
ICE	Intercontinental Commodity Exchange
ICO	International Coffee Organisation
IACO	Inter-African Coffee Organisation
Kg	Kilogramme
MICE	Melbourne International Coffee Expo
MPI	Multidimensional Poverty Index
MY	Marketing Year
NCA	National Coffee Association
NCDT	National Coffee Drinking Trends

NZSCA	New Zealand Specialty Coffee Association
SCA	Specialty Coffee Association
SCAJ	Specialty Coffee Association of Japan
SCTA	Swiss Coffee Traders Association
SDGs	Sustainable Development Goals (of the United Nations)
UAE	United Arab Emirates
UCDA	Uganda Coffee Development Authority
UDHR	Universal Declaration of Human Rights (of the United Nations)
UK	United Kingdom
UN	United Nations Organisation
UNDP	United Nations Development Programme
US	United States (of America)
USAID	United States Agency for International Development
USDA	United States Department of Agriculture
WCPF	World Coffee Producers Forum

Introduction

This book is written for ordinary people who want to know more about the world's favourite beverage and the situation of the people who produce it. The author hopes this book will appeal to a broad spectrum of people interested in coffee or are curious about the context within which this beverage should be understood. The author apologises in advance for any technical language that may seep through but hopes that the book will stir some interest in coffee, and shed light on areas that might not have been so obvious to ordinary consumers. For more than two decades, there has been increasing concern about the livelihoods of people engaged in food production, what their conditions are and whether they receive a fair reward for their efforts. Coffee, the second most globally traded commodity after oil, has been the centre of the discussion and engagement, primarily because of the smallholder farmers who produce it in some of the world's poorest countries.

Someone once said, "When you buy something, you put money in people's pockets and give them dignity for their skills." The people who consume coffee effectively contribute to putting money in the pockets of various people in the value chain. However, the question that lingers on is how to ensure the dignity of the people who grow the coffee! This beverage is a favourite to many all over the globe. From sweltering desert conditions to icy cold environments, coffee lovers share the same passion: for an espresso, a latte, mocha, cappuccino, Frappuccino, Americano, and others. Coffee is consumed widely as a hot beverage. However, it is also presented as a cold brew or iced coffee. In some markets, it may be dispensed in the same way as cold beverages like beers, sodas and fruit drinks, whether coin-operated, credit/debit card swiped or otherwise. Suffice it to say a culture surrounds coffee worldwide, with variances between producing and consuming countries.

Coffee influences social cohesion, business and a global culture that brings many interests together. It has a reputation as one of the world's most widely consumed beverages which, though affected somewhat during the COVID-19 lockdowns, seems to have made significant recovery. Over a four-year stretch, 2019-2023, there were significant shifts in the global coffee markets from the pre-COVID to the post-COVID period. The lockdowns in different countries spurred an increase in coffee deliveries to customers. They led to a surge in at-home consumption in some markets as out-of-home consumption significantly decreased due to movement restrictions. There were different innovations where coffee outlets, cafes, and others introduced new ways of serving customers. The summation of all of these contributed to historical highs in demand for coffee, partially attributed to the COVID-related trends whose effect on the market was increased consumption. Nonetheless, per capita consumption remained high in the traditional markets, as seen in Chapter One.

The book is structured as follows:

Chapter One introduces coffee as the world's favourite beverage, highlighting global consumption and zooming in on the European and North American markets. The Nordic countries notably have a higher per capita consumption than others, followed by other European nations, with evidence of Europe's position as the most significant destination of all coffee imports from the producing countries. Chapter Two focuses on consumption in the rest of the world, covering Latin America, Asia, Oceania, and Africa — the significance of the emerging markets and the potential in those markets are noteworthy. Chapter Three focuses on Coffee and Health, and discusses various studies that show the benefits of moderate coffee drinking and advice on modest consumption based on scientific evidence.

Chapter Four discusses coffee and poverty — the hot topic. The chapter highlights the plight of the coffee producers, the unfavourable conditions under which they operate, and includes a call for action to all concerned parties. Chapter Five focuses on where the coffee is grown, pointing out the top-producing countries and how it is grown in those countries. Brazil is the top producer, and the Latin American region leads in production, accounting for almost 60% of global output. Some smaller producers are also mentioned, especially for their exceptional quality.

Chapter Six discusses coffee and culture, and explicitly highlights the Ethiopian coffee ceremony. All connoisseurs would love this encounter, which starts with roasting the beans in a clay or metallic skillet over a charcoal stove. The roast's aroma fills the room — an important Ethiopian experience. After roasting the coffee, the traditional method of getting the ground powder is by pounding the roasted beans in a mortar using a wooden pestle. Subsequently, the powder is poured into a clay pot with boiling water, which is generally left on the fire, and from which the beverage is served in small round cups. It is also ensured that coffee keeps brewing in the pot as the ceremony goes on so all those present can drink as much as they want. The coffee cultures in the different countries are mentioned and discussed. However, there is a discussion on the origins of both Arabica and Robusta, the two commonest varieties, explicitly focusing on Ethiopia as the origin of Arabica coffee and Uganda as the origin of Robusta and the Buganda coffee culture.

Chapter Seven discusses the genesis of the World Coffee Producers Forum as the producers' initiative to address farmers' global plight and what it has achieved. Chapter Eight looks at some innovations that could increase producers' earnings. These are not exhaustive but give a glimpse of some current actions, acknowledging that there is much more to do to address poverty among coffee producers. Chapter Nine discusses a few transformational ideas and their potential impact on the global industry. Chapter Ten handles the proposed path to prosperity for producers. In contrast, Chapter Eleven discusses some emerging issues that the producers closely follow and watch. Chapter Twelve narrates the author's story and coffee experience, which provided the background to the writing of this book.

Frederick S. M. Kawuma, PhD
Author
17th January 2024

1

The World's Favourite Beverage — Consumption in Europe and North America

In its overview of the global industry for the 2021/22 coffee year, the International Coffee Organization (ICO) noted that global consumption had increased to 170.3 million 60-kg bags from 164.9 million in the previous year. The increase of around 3.3% was significant, considering the global economic rebound after the dampening effects of the COVID-19 pandemic. The war in Ukraine, coming hot on the heels of the pandemic, also impacted consumption as it complicated access to a popular beverage.

Despite the attendant challenges, coffee can find its way into the hands of consumers globally. Moreover, the industry is regularly coming up with innovative new methods of brewing and serving coffee, in addition to various promotions in the different markets, which all account for the yearly increase in consumption. One might ask, 'How many people drink coffee?' Estimates indicate that over one billion people drink coffee daily, with an average of 2.25 billion cups consumed worldwide.

Most of the consumption is in the form of roasted and ground coffee, but it is also noteworthy that there is an increasing consumption of instant coffee. There is a revolution in the market in producing and consuming countries because of significant improvements in instant coffee. The change has to do with the innovations and reinventions that have greatly enhanced its quality. Estimates indicate that instant coffee corresponds to nearly 25 per cent of global coffee consumption, with a growth of 2.5 to 3 per cent per year, higher than the traditional roasted coffee, whose growth has been in the region of 2 per cent per annum for a while.

Global innovations are constantly bringing new coffee brands of all forms of coffee into the market. One of the world's most popular brands is Starbucks, which has grown to become the world's largest coffee retailer and undeniably tops the list of the best brand in consumers' minds worldwide. Headquartered in Seattle, USA, it was founded in 1971 but had its turnaround after its acquisition by one of its employees, Howard Shultz, in the 1980s, and progressively its trajectory changed dramatically. Starbucks' operations span more than 33,800 stores in 80 countries. Undoubtedly, Starbucks caused significant disruption in the retail coffee business in the US, then across the rest of the developed world, and into the emerging markets, growing into a recognisable brand in all major global cities.

However, the developed consumer markets have some strict legal and non-legal requirements regarding what they allow in, with the bar much higher for processed coffee. These regulations mainly apply to primary or extra food safety certification and sustainability standards. Also, coffee that meets high compliance standards with specific niche requirements or exceptionally high sustainability and quality thresholds may have increased chances of access to some markets. Such coffee may command higher prices/values, though the volumes are lower than those on the conventional market.

Europe is the leading destination and the leader in consumption, accounting for about one-third of global consumption. The US is also an important market and the biggest importer as a country, though much lower than Europe in per capita consumption. Over 150 million people in America consume coffee daily, and almost one-third of adults above 18.

Despite the US's reputation as the number one importer, Worldatlas.com, in 2024, ranked it only 25th on the list of biggest consumers! As we will see later, the Nordic countries lead in per capita consumption. Worldatlas statistics indicated that Nordic countries consumed up to 8-12 kg per person annually. A disclaimer stated that some of the referenced figures were based on statistics collected two to three years earlier, and the rankings could change, but the general consumption trend was positive in most markets. However, the International Coffee Organization released the top per capita consumption statistics for 2022, as shown in the following table.

Top Global Per Capita Coffee Consumption Ranking in 2022			
Consumption Ranking	Country	Per capita consumption in lbs	Per capita consumption in kgs
1.	Finland	23.1	10.5
2.	Sweden	20.1	9.1
3.	Belgium	19.8	9.0
4.	Norway	18.5	8.4
5.	Iceland	18.1	8.2
6.	Switzerland	17.9	8.1
7.	Brunei Darussalam	17.6	8.0
8.	Denmark	16.8	7.6
9.	Austria	16.3	7.4
10.	Costa Rica	15.4	7.0
11.	Netherlands	15.2	6.9
12.	Canada	14.8	6.7
13.	Lithuania	14.8	6.7
14.	Cyprus	14.6	6.6
15.	Germany	14.6	6.6
16.	Cayman Islands	14.3	6.5
17.	Greece	14.1	6.4
18.	Brazil	14.1	6.4
19.	Israel	13.9	6.3

Source: *International Coffee Organization*

Europe

Europe is recognised as a long-standing traditional market for coffee and accounted for 33% of global consumption in the 2020/21 season. The European Coffee Federation, in their 2022/2023 Report, indicated that in 2022 the 27 member states of the European Union accounted for imports of about 2.948 million tonnes (49.128 million 60-kg bags), and the total for all of Europe was 3.156 million tonnes (55.92 million 60-kg bags) The above reality makes Europe the most significant coffee market in the world. Europe also has the most extensive coffee roasting capacities, led by Germany, Italy, Spain, the Netherlands and France. The EU takes the premier position for the world's highest per capita consumption, even though this varies from country to country, and the countries of Europe account for one out of three coffee consumers globally. The EU is a significant destination from all producing regions and is especially critical for Africa. Western Europe has the highest average annual consumption at approximately 6 kg per capita, and the Nordic countries are Europe's biggest per capita coffee drinkers. The German-speaking countries of Germany, Austria and Switzerland also consume a significant amount, led by Germany. Bosnia and Montenegro have also become very important to exporters due to their increasing consumption.

Nordic Countries

The Nordic countries are seriously in love with coffee. Consumption is exceptionally high, and they are renowned for their love of a beverage that plays a significant role in people's culture and daily routines. Consumption habits reflect a deep appreciation for quality coffee and a solid coffee-drinking tradition. Nordic countries, including Finland, Sweden, Norway, and Denmark, consistently rank among the top consuming nations in the world. Deeply ingrained in the social fabric, it is common for people to meet friends, family, or colleagues for a coffee break, which serves as a social ritual for bonding and conversation. Such breaks are seen as essential moments to relax and connect with others. The Nordic countries have a strong tradition of brewing and enjoying 'filter' coffee. The "Nordic-style" often involves using high-quality, locally roasted beans and a slow extraction process. Brewing methods like the drip brew or pour-over are popular, showcasing the coffee's nuanced flavours and aromas.

Nordic households often have brewing equipment, and many people prefer to brew and enjoy coffee in the comfort of their own space. Home brewing methods like drip coffee makers, French press, and Aeropress are popular choices. These countries of northern Europe host various coffee-related events, competitions, and festivals. The events celebrate coffee culture, provide platforms for baristas to showcase their skills, and offer opportunities for enthusiasts to explore new trends and products. There are variations in individual consumption habits within different regions of Nordic countries. Nonetheless, the coffee culture in this society is characterised by high consumption, an emphasis on quality, and the significance of coffee in social and cultural contexts.

The Nordic countries strongly focus on quality, and specialty coffee is highly valued. Specialty shops and roasters are abundant, offering a wide range of single-origin beans, specialty blends, and alternative brewing methods. Baristas in Nordic countries often have extensive knowledge and expertise in coffee preparation. The concept of 'fika' is central to coffee culture in Nordic countries, particularly in Sweden. *Fika* refers to a coffee break accompanied by pastries or snacks. It is a cherished tradition that encourages people to take a break, relax, and enjoy coffee and treats together.

Finland is the world's biggest consumer per person, where the average Finn consumes nearly four cups a day. ICO figures for 2022 indicate that per capita consumption is around 10.5 kg (or 23.1 lbs) annually. The popularity in Finland is so incredible that there is a legal mandate of two 10-minute coffee breaks for Finnish workers. Closely following Finland, the Nordic neighbour Sweden is another high consumer. Swedes consume 9.1 kilos (20.1 lbs) per capita annually, which is significant given a population of 10 million. Belgium edged in between the Nordic consumers, ahead of Norway, where the per capita consumption is 9.0 kg (or 19.8 lbs). Norway is in fourth position, with per capita consumption of 8.4 kilos (18.4 lbs). Norwegians reportedly drink more than three cups daily. Norway is closely followed by Iceland, recorded by the ICO as number five in per capita consumption of 8.2 kilos (18.1 lbs)

Norway and Finland have populations between five and six million. As it made its way around the world, coffee's introduction to the Scandinavians in the 1600s only gained popularity in Sweden in the 1700s, and they fell in love with it. The Swedes love warm drinks — including coffee. Coffee is part and parcel of Swedish culture, and nearly three centuries ago, the government was so concerned about its popularity and how much Swedish revenue was moving abroad to buy coffee, that the beverage was banned. The joke is that since coffee was banned in 1756, when hefty fines were imposed on consumption until finally allowed and legalised in 1823, the Swedish drank as much as they could, just in case it was banned again, and the coffee-drinking tradition has since held. The Swedish market is vibrant and gives much hope to coffee entrepreneurs, especially since Sweden is more populous than the other Nordic countries.

Belgium

Belgium is the third-largest importer in Europe, and ranked by the ICO as the third top consumer. Consumption is significant, and coffee holds a special place in the country's culinary traditions. Belgians have a reputation for high coffee consumption, have a rich coffee culture and enjoy a variety of coffee preparations. According to Statista, from 2019 data, coffee beans were Belgium's most popular coffee type, responsible for approximately half of the coffee sales, while instant coffee and filter coffee were markedly less prevalent, with market shares of roughly 12 and two per cent, respectively. Belgians have a strong affinity for coffee. ICO's data showed that Belgium's average annual per capita consumption had increased from around 6 to 7 kilograms reported by Statista in 2019 to 9 kilos (19.8 lbs) in 2022. Belgium is known for its unique coffee specialties. One famous example is the "Café Liégeois," a cold dessert made with layers of coffee-flavoured ice cream, whipped cream, and chocolate sauce. Another specialty is the "Mokatine," a coffee-flavoured praline filled with a creamy coffee centre.

Belgium has a thriving café culture, with numerous coffee houses and cafés scattered across cities and towns. These establishments provide cosy and inviting spaces for people to enjoy their coffee, meet friends, and indulge in pastries or chocolates. While traditional filter coffee is consumed, espresso-based drinks are popular in Belgium. Cappuccinos, lattes, and macchiatos are commonly enjoyed, often served with artistic foam designs or chocolate sprinkles.

Belgium has witnessed the rise of specialty coffee in recent years. Specialty coffee shops and roasters have emerged, offering high-quality beans, single-origin coffees, and alternative brewing methods. Belgian baristas know increasingly about coffee sourcing, roasting techniques, and flavour profiles.

Belgium has its coffee brands and artisanal roasters known for their expertise in creating unique blends and roasting techniques. Companies like Rombouts and Belmoca are well-established Belgian coffee brands offering a range of products for both home and commercial use. Many Belgians also prefer to enjoy coffee at home. Home coffee machines, such as espresso makers or filter coffee machines, are standard in Belgian households, allowing individuals to brew their preferred coffee and experiment with different flavours and preparations.

Belgium is renowned for its chocolate, and the combination of coffee and chocolate is highly valued. Its people often savour a cup of coffee alongside a piece of high-quality Belgian chocolate, creating a delightful pairing of flavours. As already noted with other countries, consumption habits can vary among individuals and regions within Belgium. On the whole, Belgium's coffee culture is characterised by a love for coffee specialities, a thriving café scene, and an appreciation for quality coffee.

Switzerland

Switzerland closely follows Belgium, with a significant capita consumption of 8.1 kg (17.9 lbs). Switzerland is known to be the global centre of coffee trading, hosting most of the significant traders and roasters. According to the Swiss Coffee Traders Association (SCTA), coffee represents one third of drinks consumed daily in Swiss canteens, cafes, and restaurants. It accounts for nearly 10 per cent of the turnover of Swiss restaurants and coffee outlets — the Swiss drink 1,110 cups of coffee per person per year, thus roughly three cups per day.

Switzerland has a rich coffee culture, and consumption is quite popular. Swiss people are known for their appreciation of high-quality coffee and often prioritise the taste and experience of preparation. It is no wonder that Switzerland consistently ranks among the top countries in consumption per capita. According to data from the International Coffee Organization, Switzerland's per capita consumption is relatively high, ranking seventh worldwide in 2020, with an annual average of around 7 to 8 kilograms consumed per person and growing. The specialty coffee movement also took the Swiss by storm, and Switzerland has a growing specialty scene focusing on high-quality and artisanal coffee.

In all the major cities, specialty coffee shops and cafes are abundant, where trained baristas serve a variety of single-origin coffees, specialty blends, and carefully crafted espresso-based drinks. Coffee is an integral part of Swiss culture, and it is common for people to meet and socialise over a cup of coffee. Swiss cafes and coffee houses provide a cosy and inviting atmosphere for locals and tourists alike to enjoy their coffee, whether a quick espresso or a leisurely break. Swiss drinkers prefer espresso-based drinks like cappuccinos, lattes, and macchiatos. Swiss baristas are skilled in preparing these beverages with precision and attention to detail, often creating latte art designs on the surface of the milk foam.

Swiss households often have coffee machines or espresso makers to enjoy coffee at home. Many people prefer to have a cup of coffee in the morning or after a meal in the comfort of their homes. Switzerland has local coffee brands, such as Mövenpick,

Delica AG, Café Royal, Chicco d'Oro and Jura, offering a range of home and commercial products. International brands are also widely available in supermarkets and specialty stores. Switzerland hosts various coffee events and festivals, showcasing the latest trends, equipment, and products in the industry. These events attract enthusiasts, professionals, and the general public interested in exploring the world of coffee. However, consumption habits can vary among individuals, and preferences may differ in different regions of Switzerland, albeit the overall coffee culture in the country reflects a high appreciation for quality and a solid coffee-drinking tradition.

Germany

Germany is the biggest importer of coffee in Europe, ranks among Europe's top consumers, and is perhaps Europe's most significant market, where coffee is the most consumed beverage. Consumption is significant, and coffee is prominent in the country's culture and daily routines. In Germany's foods and drinks sector, coffee is one of the country's most appreciated energy boosts. Millions of Germans start their morning with a cup as a ritual. Tentative statistics in 2021 indicated that Germany's per capita consumption was 169 litres per annum, specifically about 6.5 kg per person, with a slight increase to 6.6 kilos (14.6 lbs) in 2022, according to the ICO. Although below that of Norway and Finland, this is significant because of its greater population. Strong demand for freshly brewed coffee is responsible for Germany's growth in consumption. Reports indicate that many Germans have coffee machines for office or home consumption, with more than 1 out of four Germans aged between 18 and 29 having or aspiring to have a machine. The aspiration among young consumers is a good sign of future growth in the market.

Coffee is often an essential part of the morning routine for many Germans. It is common for people to start their day with a cup, either at home or at cafes, before heading to work or engaging in daily activities. Germany has a vibrant café culture, particularly in cities like Berlin, Bonn, Munich, and Hamburg. Cafes serve as social spaces where people can enjoy a cup, meet friends, have business meetings, or simply relax. German cafes often offer a variety of coffee specialities and pastries. Filter coffee, brewed using various methods such as drip brewing or French press, is widely consumed.

Additionally, espresso-based drinks like cappuccinos, lattes, and espressos are popular choices, and Germans appreciate well-prepared coffee focusing on taste and quality. Home equipment, including automatic coffee makers and espresso machines, are standard in German households, which allows individuals to prepare their preferred drink anytime and offers convenience and flexibility.

Germany has a long-standing tradition of coffee houses, particularly in cities with cultural significance like Hamburg and Berlin. These establishments offer a cosy atmosphere and a wide selection of coffee beverages, pastries, and cakes. *Kaffee und Kuchen* (coffee and cake) is a cherished German tradition, which typically involves enjoying a slice of cake, pastry, and coffee, especially in the afternoon. It is a social occasion where friends and family gather to savour sweet treats and have conversations over coffee. Germany has brands and roasters offering a range of products, and well-known German coffee brands include Tchibo, Jacobs, Dallmayr, and Eduscho.

Additionally, specialty coffee shops and artisanal roasters have also gained popularity, catering to those seeking high-quality and unique coffee experiences. While consumption habits vary among individuals and regions, coffee is significant in German culture and is appreciated for its flavour, social aspects, and contribution to daily routines.

Italy

Italy is Europe's second-largest importer of green coffee after Germany. Consumption is deeply ingrained in the country's culture and is a cherished part of daily life. It is no wonder that many brands worldwide have the label of 'Italian coffee', though Italy is not a coffee-growing country. It is famous as the place of innovations from where we got the *espresso* and *latte*, and where George Schultz of Starbucks got inspired to introduce the Italian espresso habits that fanned the specialty coffee explosion in the US. In addition to the domestic market, Italy is a critical roasted coffee supplier to other European countries, and is synonymous with espresso, the most common way Italians enjoy coffee. Espresso is a strong, concentrated shot of coffee served in a small cup. Italians typically consume espresso in quick sips while standing at a coffee bar or counter. There is a global appreciation of Italian espresso blends.

Coffee shops, known as "bar" in Italy, are central to the Italian experience. These establishments are social hubs where people gather to enjoy coffee, socialise, and catch up with friends. Italians often visit their local bar multiple times a day for a quick espresso or a *cappuccino.* Alongside espresso, Italians also enjoy other traditional coffee beverages. A cappuccino — consisting of equal parts espresso, steamed milk, and milk foam, is a popular choice for breakfast. Other favourites include caffè latte (coffee with more milk), macchiato (espresso with a dash of milk), and caffè corretto (espresso "corrected" with a small amount of alcohol). Italians have specific rituals and etiquette when it comes to coffee. It is common for locals to stand at the bar while consuming their espresso, as sitting is often associated with a more leisurely experience.

Additionally, ordering milky coffee beverages like cappuccino after morning hours is considered unusual, as it is traditionally deemed a breakfast drink. While coffee bars are integral to Italian coffee culture, many Italians enjoy their cup at home. Moka pots, stovetop espresso makers, are commonly used for brewing espresso-like coffee in the family house. It allows individuals to recreate the coffee bar experience in their kitchens.

Italians place a strong emphasis on quality. The art of coffee preparation, including selecting high-quality beans, proper extraction, and skilful espresso-making techniques, is highly valued. Italian baristas are often trained extensively to ensure the perfect espresso is served. Italy has a rich tradition of roasting, with several well-established roasters in the country. Italian coffee has a characteristically darker roast profile, which lends a robust and intense flavour to the espresso. Italian brands like L'avazza, Illy, and Segafredo are well-known globally, with substantial brand influence and a significant presence in Italy. These brands offer a wide range of products, including ground coffee, coffee capsules, and coffee beans. While this is a general account of Italian consumption, habits vary among individuals and regions within the country. Notably, a passion for espresso is characteristic of the coffee culture, emphasising quality and enjoyment as a social and cultural experience.

France

France is a significant coffee importer in Europe. It has a long coffee consumption tradition deeply ingrained in the country's culture, and coffee plays a significant role in daily life. France has a rich heritage, and coffee is enjoyed with a certain level of sophistication and style. It is one of Europe's large and mature coffee markets, holding an important position in European green coffee imports, with the Port of Le Havre as the main entry point for green coffee. The world's largest coffee roasters, Nestlé and Jacobs Douwe Egberts, have a significant presence in France, as are Lavazza and Segafredo Zanetti. Reports indicate that 68% of French people are regular coffee drinkers, although 14% never drink the beverage. French drinkers love the beverage primarily for the taste (74%), to take a break (47%), to feel better (35%), or to stay awake (33%). More than one in two French people (55%) drink coffee several times daily at home (at home or with friends and family).

Coffee's special place in French culture means that enjoying the beverage is often seen as a ritual. It is common for people to take a break during the day to savour a cup and engage in conversation or relaxation. France has a vibrant café culture, particularly in cities like Paris (and, of course, the word 'cafe' is originally in French). Cafés are essential social spaces where people gather to enjoy coffee, read newspapers, or engage in lively discussions. French cafés often have outdoor seating, allowing people to enjoy coffee while observing the bustling street life. France is one of the leading consumers of decaffeinated coffee in Europe. Many French people enjoy decaf coffee after meals or in the evening to satisfy their cravings without the stimulating effects of caffeine.

France's vibrant café culture is evident in several cities, including Paris, Lyon, Nice, Marseille, Bordeaux, Aix-en-Provence and Toulouse. In Paris, Café de Flore, Les Deux Magots, and Café de la Rotonde are iconic cafés that have a rich history and are frequented by locals and tourists alike. Lyon, the gastronomic capital of France, also has a thriving café culture, and is home to numerous cafés that offer various coffee options, from traditional espresso to specialty brews. Places like Café Sillon, Café Comptoir Abel, and Café Mokxa are popular destinations. Nice is another city famous for its cafés. The picturesque city on the French Riviera is known for its charming cafés and stunning coastal views. The Promenade des Anglais and the Old Town (Vieux Nice) are dotted with cafés where visitors can relax with a cup of coffee while enjoying the Mediterranean ambience.

Marseille, a vibrant port city in southern France, has a lively café scene. The city offers a mix of traditional cafés and trendy coffee shops. The Cours Julien neighbourhood is trendy for its café culture, with many establishments serving specialty coffees and fostering a creative atmosphere. Bordeaux, renowned for its wine, also has a notable café culture. The city's charming squares and streets are adorned with cafés, where residents and visitors can unwind and savour a cup. The Place du Parlement, Place du Palais, and the Saint-Pierre district are known for their café terraces and vibrant atmosphere. Aix-en-Provence, located in the Provence region of southern France, is celebrated for its café culture. The city's elegant boulevards and picturesque squares are lined with cafés offering a wide range of coffee options. The Cours Mirabeau and the Place des Cardeurs are popular spots to enjoy a cup while taking in the charming surroundings. Finally, Toulouse, known as the "Pink City" due to its distinct architectural style, has a thriving café culture. The city offers a mix of traditional cafés, modern coffee shops, and trendy establishments. The Place du Capitole and the Rue des Filatiers are popular areas for cafés with inviting atmospheres. All the above cities, among others, exemplify the rich café culture that France has to offer. Each city has its unique charm, ambience, and café traditions, providing visitors and locals with diverse and delightful coffee experiences.

France's most popular coffee choices are café espresso and café crème (espresso with a small amount of milk). French espresso tends to be strong and intense in flavour. Café crème resembles a cappuccino but has a more significant milk proportion. In France, coffee is often enjoyed in the morning as part of the breakfast ritual. A common practice is to dunk a croissant or a piece of baguette in coffee, savouring the combination of flavours. French people value the quality of their coffee. It is common for households to have coffee machines or espresso makers at home. French drinkers appreciate well-prepared brews with a focus on taste and aroma. While traditional espresso is prevalent, a growing interest in single-origin and specialty coffees exists in France. Specialty shops and roasters have gained popularity, offering a wide range of beans, brewing methods, and flavour profiles. The concept of a coffee break, known as *"pause-café"* or *"pause-café gourmand,"* is cherished in France. It refers to taking a short break during the day to enjoy a cup, often accompanied by a small pastry or a sweet treat. It is important to note that consumption habits can vary among individuals and regions within France. However, the overall coffee culture in France emphasises the enjoyment of the beverage as a moment of relaxation, social interaction, and appreciation for the rich flavours and aromas of a well-prepared cup.

France's roasting industry is well-established and has brands with a strong presence in the European market. The French market has heralded sustainability issues for a long time, with certification being a critical requirement for buyers with a presence in this market. Thus, certified coffee is widely available in most outlets. The European specialty coffee movement, which started in the Nordic countries in the 1990s, has taken shape in France and offers significant opportunities to producers who can provide high-quality coffees with unique stories. However, the volume of specialty coffees is small (less than 5%) compared to the mainstream, though projected to grow to 10 per cent in the next few years. For decades, there has been much talk about imitating the French terroir concept in promoting specialty coffees to copy from the age-old French wine sector, with stories highlighting the origin, production and preparation methods and quality distinctions. Linked to this is a drive, headed by the Agency for the Valorization of Agricultural Products (AVPA), based in Paris, to highlight exceptional coffees from different countries and promote coffee roasted at different places of origin and then distributed by partners in France.

The United Kingdom

Interestingly, although the United Kingdom (UK) prides itself as a nation of coffee lovers, it does not feature among ICO's top-ranked 19 coffee-consuming countries, as it historically had a conservative tea-consuming culture. Nonetheless, London has been at the centre of coffee trading in Europe for centuries, hosting both the headquarters of the International Coffee Organization (ICO) and the London Coffee Exchange (LCE) that initially traded in Robusta. The LCE morphed into various entities through six decades and no longer has its original identity but now trades under the Intercontinental Commodity Exchange (ICE). London has been at the centre of international coffee diplomacy, and during the period when quotas directed global coffee trading, several meetings were held in London throughout the year to negotiate and allocate the quotas to both producing and consuming countries.

The UK has over 30,000 cafes, coffee shops, and other coffee-serving venues. The coffee shop business is estimated to be worth £15 billion a year, making it a significant contributor to the British economy. UK consumers mostly prefer white beverages (latte, cappuccino, and the like). In contrast, a more significant proportion of consumers in the rest of Europe prefer an unadulterated form. The British Coffee Association reports consumption of approximately 98 million cups per day in the UK, on average, where 65 per cent is consumed at home, 25 per cent consumed at work or whilst studying, with the remaining 10 per cent consumed in coffee shops, bars and restaurants. The oldest known café in Europe is Queen's Lane Coffee House in Oxford, England, allegedly founded in 1654.

Coffee consumption in the UK has been on a steady rise in recent years, reflecting its growing popularity as the preferred hot beverage among the British population. This trend can be attributed to the influence of coffee shop chains, increased awareness of specialty coffee, and a shift in consumer tastes. The UK has a vibrant culture, particularly in cities like London, Edinburgh, and Manchester. Coffee shops — both independent and chain establishments like Costa Coffee, Starbucks, and Caffè Nero — offer various coffee options and serve as social spaces for people to meet, work, or relax.

Espresso-based drinks like cappuccinos, lattes, and flat whites are popular. These beverages are widely available in coffee shops and are often customised with different milk options, flavours, or latte art. An increasing number of independent coffee shops and artisanal roasters focus on sourcing high-quality beans, emphasising craftsmanship, and offering unique flavour profiles. Specialty coffee enthusiasts check out these establishments for their expertise and distinct experiences. With the rise of warmer weather and changing tastes, cold brew and iced coffee have gained popularity. Many coffee shops now offer cold brew options and refreshing iced beverages during summer.

While specialty coffee is gaining popularity, instant coffee still holds a significant market share in the UK. Instant is convenient and often consumed at home or the workplace, allowing quick and easy preparation. Many Britons enjoy coffee at home, with coffee machines and espresso makers being common kitchen appliances. Brewing methods like French press, pour-over, and AeroPress are also embraced by enthusiasts who prefer to prepare their brew to specific taste preferences. The popularity of coffee pods and capsules, such as those used in Nespresso or Keurig machines, has increased. These single-serving coffee options provide convenience and a variety of flavours for those seeking a quick and hassle-free experience.

The UK has a growing number of local roasters and micro-roasteries, though the roasting scale cannot be compared to that in Germany, Italy, France or the Netherlands. UK roasters focus on sourcing ethically and sustainably produced beans from worldwide regions. They cater to the demand for specialty coffee and offer unique flavour profiles to enthusiasts. Consumption habits vary among individuals and regions within the UK, but the country's overall coffee culture reflects a growing appreciation for specialty coffee. In addition, a thriving coffee shop scene and a mix of traditional and modern consumption habits punctuate the British consumption culture.

Top Brands in Europe

In 2020, Costa Coffee was ranked, by Statista, as Europe's leading coffee shop chain, with 3,148 units across Europe. The other chains were McCafé and Starbucks which took second and third place, respectively. With regard to products, the French brand Carte Noire which is the same name as the company itself was identified as one of the best European brands. This French brand offers a range of products that include whole-bean, ground, instant, and coffee pods. The company's way of blending pure Arabica beans is noted to create a luxurious flavour, which is one of the reasons why it has earned the number-one spot as a top European brand. Other favourite European brands have been named as Dallmayr Prodomo Ground Coffee, Leroux, Jacques Vabre, Jacobs Kronung Whole Bean Coffee, Legal Le Gout, Grand'mère, Eduscho Gala Nr. 1 Ground Coffee, Barissimo Ground Coffee, Tchibo Feine Milde Ground Coffee, Illy Classico Whole Bean Coffee, and Lavazza Gran Espresso Whole Bean Coffee Blend.

Consumption in North America

North America is an important traditional market, which has been a primary driver of the specialty coffee movement, with Starbucks as a critical player. Northern America region consists of the United States, Canada, and Mexico, and the dependencies of St. Pierre and Miquelon, Greenland, and Bermuda. The largest country is Canada, though its population is much less than that of the US, the latter being the single biggest consumer of coffee as a country, and accounting for about 20 per cent of global imports. At the time of writing, Mexico was not a significant consumer but primarily a producing country. The discussion of Mexico's consumption is included in the section covering consumption in Latin American countries.

The United States

Surveys indicate that at least three out of every five adults in the US consume coffee daily. In addition, reports indicate that over 150 million US consumers drink about 400 million cups daily.

Altogether, on an annual basis, the US consumes about 146 billion cups of coffee. Almost four of every five US consumers prepare their beverage at home, indicating the importance of at-home consumption. Another interesting statistic is that at least one in three US consumers usually drinks black coffee, indicating a tendency to appreciate the flavour. Starbucks is credited for influencing US consumers toward a more potent drink than before, which was critical at the outset of the US specialty coffee movement in the 1980s and has persisted.

For logistical reasons, the US is a significant market for Latin American producers because of its proximity. However, produce from Africa and Asia also finds some critical inroads. Since the 1980s, an increasing demand for higher-quality coffees has been noted as consumers became more aware and sophisticated. In addition, there has been an increasing trend of cause-related marketing and attention to factors such as organic, fair trade, bird-friendly, rain-forest-friendly coffee, and other social and environmental concerns and a proliferation of labels associated with these causes. Different specialty brands from the producers south of the USA have found their niches among American consumers.

The US has a vibrant and diverse consumption culture that has evolved over time. Coffee is deeply ingrained in American society and plays a significant role in daily life for many people. It is often seen as an essential part of the morning routine for many Americans. It is common practice to start the day with a cup of coffee to help wake up and prepare for the day ahead. The US has experienced significant growth in the specialty coffee movement in recent years. There is an increased focus on high-quality coffee, artisanal brewing methods, and an appreciation for the nuances of different origins, flavours, and brewing techniques.

Coffee shops or cafés have become social hubs in many communities, offering a place to meet, work, study, or relax. Coffee shops provide a variety of options, including espresso-based drinks, pour-over brews, and flavoured specialty beverages, catering to diverse preferences. Americans often enjoy customisation and variety when it comes to their coffee choices. Many shops offer a wide range of milk options, flavoured syrups, and additional toppings, allowing individuals to personalise their coffee. Due to busy lifestyles and on-the-go activities, takeaway or "to-go" coffee culture is prominent in the US. Many people opt for convenient options, such as coffee served in disposable cups, drive-through stands, or mobile carts. Single-serve coffee machines, particularly the Keurig system, have gained popularity as they allow individuals to brew a single cup of coffee quickly and easily, offering convenience and variety.

The US hosts various coffee-related events, including coffee festivals, competitions, and trade shows, where industry professionals and enthusiasts come together to share knowledge, showcase products, and celebrate the coffee culture. The Specialty Coffee Exposition, hosted by the Specialty Coffee Association, is one of the world's biggest annual coffee events drawing over 30,000 people. Overall, the US coffee consumption culture is dynamic, diverse, and influenced by a combination of traditional brewing methods, evolving trends, and a growing appreciation for specialty coffee. Whether enjoyed at home, in shops, or on the go, coffee holds a special place in American daily life and social interactions.

Canada

Canada is an important market that has grown in consumption over the last few decades, and it is the only one of the top ten consuming countries not located in Europe. According to the International Coffee Organization, Canada had a yearly consumption of 3.9 million (60kg bags) in 2018 — behind the EU, the US, Japan and Russia. However, Canada's imports grew to over 5 million bags by the end of 2022. Surprisingly, Canada is one of the largest consumers in the world, ranking ahead of the US, with 6.7 kg (14.8 lbs) per capita consumption, compared with America's about 4.4 kg (9.7 lbs) per capita.

Interestingly, Canada tends to be overshadowed by the US because of its relatively smaller population size and comparatively lower volume of imports. However, Canada is, in fact, a significant market, and in 2021 the most consumption was noted to be among those aged 25 to 44 years, with the age group of 35- to 44-year-olds notably having the highest share of coffee drinkers. The Coffee Association of Canada reports that two in three Canadians enjoy at least one cup daily, averaging 3.2 cups per day. Coffee shops are popular gathering places, providing a space for socialising, working, or studying. Canadian coffee chains, such as Tim Hortons, Second Cup, and Blenz Coffee, are well-known and widely frequented. Independent shops also thrive, offering specialty coffee, artisanal brewing methods, and a cosy atmosphere. Tim Hortons, one of the world's top chains, which debuted in Canada, has a ubiquitous presence and is reputed to make three out of every four cups sold in Canada. Tim Hortons holds a special place in Canadian culture. It is an iconic Canadian coffee and doughnut chain that has become a part of Canadian identity. Tim Hortons' locations can be found throughout the country, and many Canadians have a fondness for their offerings.

Similar to the US culture, Canadians often start their day with a cup, and it is common for individuals to have their preferred morning coffee routine, whether brewing at home or stopping by a local café. There has been a growing appreciation for specialty coffee in Canada in recent years. Independent shops and roasters that focus on high-quality beans, sustainable sourcing, and skilled baristas have gained popularity, particularly in urban centres. Like in the US, Canadians also embrace the convenience of "to-go" coffee culture. Many coffee shops offer takeaway options, drive-throughs, and mobile trucks to cater to busy lifestyles and on-the-go activities. Canadians often embrace seasonal coffee flavours and beverages. During the fall and winter, there is a demand for spiced coffees, pumpkin spice lattes, and other warm and cosy flavours. In the summer, iced coffees and cold brews become popular choices to beat the heat.

Canadians have shown an increased interest in sustainability and ethical sourcing practices in the coffee industry. Many shops and consumers prioritise fair trade, organic, and locally sourced beans, supporting sustainable practices and supporting coffee-growing communities. The consumption culture in Canada is diverse, reflecting a mix of traditional preferences, a growing interest in specialty coffee, and a love for socialising over a cup of the beverage. It is an integral part of Canadian daily life and offers a sense of comfort, community, and enjoyment.

Conclusion

Europe and North America have been the traditional markets over many decades. However, some European countries are not included among the significant consumers but are considered part of the emerging market, including the nations of the former Soviet Union. As affluence increases in those countries, consumption too is notably on the rise. Several organisations provide specific reports on consumption trends in Europe and North America which include the International Coffee Organization (ICO),

European Coffee Federation (ECF), Euromonitor International, National Coffee Association (NCA) in both USA and Canada, Specialty Coffee Association (SCA), and Statista.

The ICO provides comprehensive data and analysis on worldwide production, consumption, and trade and publishes an annual Coffee Market Report that covers global coffee trends and statistics. The ECF represents the European industry and releases reports on various aspects of the market, including consumption trends. Though it does not provide a statistical service, its reports provide insights into coffee consumption patterns, preferences, and European market developments. Euromonitor International is a market research company that offers reports on various industries, including coffee. They provide data on coffee consumption, market size, and critical trends within different European countries. The NCA conducts surveys and publishes reports on consumption trends in the US. Their annual National Coffee Drinking Trends (NCDT) report provides insights into consumer behaviour, preferences, and market dynamics. The SCA represents the specialty coffee industry and researches consumption trends. They produce reports such as the SCA Coffee Market Snapshot, which provides an overview of the specialty market and emerging trends in North America. Statista is a leading provider of market and consumer data globally. Statista offers reports and statistics on coffee consumption globally and special coverage in North America, including information on retail sales, market size, and consumer behaviour. Reports from Statista and the above-quoted trade organisations provide valuable information on consumption trends, preferences, and market dynamics in Europe and North America, even though the availability and depth of reports may vary and there could yet be more information and reports from other organisations that are region- or country-specific to Europe and North America. The next chapter discusses consumption in the rest of the world.

2

The World's Favourite Beverage — Consumption in Latin America, Asia and Oceania, and Africa

Coffee consumption varies across the rest of the world, beyond North America and Europe. Several factors influence this consumption, including cultural preferences, economic development, and historical traditions. Following a brief overview of coffee consumption in Latin America, Oceania, and Africa, this chapter presents specific information on each region. Latin America is a region of the Americas where Romance languages — languages derived from Latin — are predominantly spoken, though the term does not have a precise definition. However, it is "commonly used to describe South America, Central America, Mexico, and the islands of the Caribbean". The Encyclopaedia Britannica gives a list of 22 countries in Latin America as the following:

Argentina	Costa Rica	Haiti	Peru
Belize	Cuba	Honduras	Puerto Rico (a territory of the United States)

Bolivia	Dominican Republic	Mexico	Uruguay
Brazil	Ecuador	Nicaragua	Venezuela
Chile	El Salvador	Panama	
Colombia	Guatemala	Paraguay	

Latin America is known for being the leading coffee-producing region worldwide — with countries like Brazil, Colombia, and Peru having a strong coffee culture and being significant exporters. In many Latin American countries, consumption is high, with a preference for freshly brewed, often more potent coffee preparations. Asia's consumption has been steadily growing in recent years. Countries such as Japan, South Korea, and China have seen a rise due to increasing urbanisation and Western influences. Instant coffee, ready-to-drink coffee, and specialty coffee shops have gained popularity.

Coffee holds cultural and social significance in the Middle East and North Africa. Turkey and Saudi Arabia have a long-standing tradition of preparing and serving such delights as Turkish coffee and Arabic coffee. Coffee preferences in these countries often include strong, rich, and sweetened preparations. While Africa is a significant coffee-producing region, consumption varies across countries. In Ethiopia, the birthplace of coffee, traditional coffee ceremonies are a cultural tradition. In East African countries and South Africa, specialty coffee shops and cafés are emerging, catering to a growing urban population with a taste for specialty coffee. Oceania, Australia and New Zealand have a well-developed culture leaning toward specialty coffee. Characteristically, these countries have many coffee shops and a preference for espresso-based beverages. Consumption in other countries in Oceania, such as Fiji and Papua New Guinea, tends to be more moderate.

Consumption patterns beyond Europe and North America have evolved. Several factors account for the changing influence of coffee, including economic development, globalisation, and changing consumer preferences. The level of consumption and the specific preferences show variations within each region and country in the rest of the world.

Consumption in Latin America

International Coffee Organisation (ICO) reports show that Latin America accounts for almost 60% of worldwide production, with modest increases in consumption. Brazil is the largest producer by far, followed by Colombia, Honduras, Peru and Mexico. In 2020, Brazil produced nearly 63 million 60-kilogram bags, representing over one-third of that year's global production, yet consuming almost a third of its own production. Colombia ranked second in the region, with almost 14 million bags produced. According to World Population Review, Brazil is the largest consumer in the region, with a total consumption of 21.5 million 60-kilogram bags in 2019. Colombia ranked second, with a total consumption of 4.5 million bags. Historically, Latin American coffee is predominantly shipped to North America and Europe. However, the last three decades to 2020 have seen increasing consumption in the Latin American region. Projections indicate that consumption in Latin America could reach 1.1 billion kilograms by 2025, with an average volume per person of 1.57 kilograms in 2023.

The per capita consumption varies widely across the region, depending on the culture and preferences of each country. According to Statista, Honduras had the highest per capita consumption in 2016, with 4.89 kilograms per person. Brazil ranked second, with 4.8 kilograms per person. Other countries with high per capita consumption were Costa Rica (4.59 kilograms), Guatemala (4.22 kilograms) and Colombia (2.8 kilograms). In 2023, the revenue in the coffee segment in Latin America was expected to amount to US$18.8 billion, with an annual growth rate of 4.59%. Brazil is the largest market in the region, with a revenue projection of US$6.8 billion in 2023. In relation to total population, revenues per capita in Latin America was US$28.88 in 2023 in Latin America. By 2025, 64% of spending and 11% of volume consumption in the coffee segment would be attributable to out-of-home consumption (e.g., in coffee bars and restaurants).

Brazil deserves special mention because it is the leader in the coffee consumption revolution among producing countries, after Ethiopia. In the 1990s, the private sector launched a programme to promote consumption, largely achieving its objectives. The project involved extensive market research to identify consumption habits, consumer preferences and product positioning. Rather than target the quick response to various stimuli, the project aimed at the long-term impact that would change habits and consumption culture, identifying interlocutors in both the private and public sectors and using opinion leaders and influencers to lead the desired change. Brazil is a contender for the top global position of the highest consumption by a country, currently held by USA.

Colombia's consumption is lower than Brazil's, at about 2.8 kg per capita, in 2023 or 2.2 million bags of green bean equivalent (GBE). That was a 40% increase from the previous year's consumption of 2.0 kg per capita. It is a recovery that brought consumption to the pre-COVID levels, a result of rapid economic recovery after the pandemic. To increase consumption, the Colombia Growers Federation launched campaigns targeting the youth and the middle class. There has been an increase in coffee shops across the country. The industry has been creating new products that satisfy the rising demand of young professionals and foreign visitors. Reports show that the bulk of the beverage consumed in Colombia is roasted and ground coffee comprising about 70% of the country's total consumption. Soluble coffee comprises the remaining 30%.

Mexico is ranked fifth globally among producers, according to the ICO. Statista says domestic consumption in Mexico was forecast to reach 2.7 million 60-kilogram bags in the coffee year 2019/20, up from nearly 2.3 million bags two years earlier. Sixty per cent of the domestic consumption was soluble coffee, while consumption of roasted ground coffee was estimated at one million bags in that year. Mexico's consumption was expected to reach around 3 million 60-kg bags by 2025. However, with a population of around 132 million, per capita consumption is significantly lower than the Latin American average, as we will see later.

According to a survey by Fredy's Tucan, Mexicans drink coffee differently depending on their region. For example, in the country's north, people prefer black coffee with sugar; in the south, they like it with cinnamon and cloves. In the centre, they add chocolate or vanilla; in the west, they drink it with milk and honey. The survey also found that every year, 32.5 billion cups are drunk in Mexico and that half of the Mexicans surveyed like to whiten their cup with a certain amount of milk or powdered cream.

In 2023, the revenue in the coffee segment was projected to be US$3.08 billion, with an annual growth rate of about 4.6% for the period 2023-2025. Considering the total population figures, the coffee segment was expected to generate average revenues of about US$23 per person in 2023. Projections indicate that by 2025, 65% of spending and 11% of volume consumption in the coffee segment would be attributable to out-of-home consumption (e.g., in bars and restaurants), a significant investment opportunity to boost the economy. Owing to its strategic position as part of the North American Free Trade Area and also the Latin American community, Mexico boasts perhaps the largest soluble coffee plant in Latin America, a significant investment by Nestle. Mexico also has one of the only decaffeination plants in Latin America.

Consumption in Asia and the Far East

Consumption in Asia dates back centuries when traders took coffee around Asia soon after its discovery in Ethiopia. According to the ICO, Asia and the Far East have experienced the most dynamic growth in consumption since 1990, growing by an average of 4% per annum, increasing to 4.9% since 2000. In 2012, the region consumed 22.5 million 60-kilogram bags, representing 13.8% of the world's total, increasing from 9.4% in 1990 to 10.9% in 2000. The largest consumers are Japan, Indonesia, South Korea, Vietnam and China. Japan alone accounted for 7.3 million bags in 2012, followed by Indonesia with 4.2 million bags. Consumption in the region is expected to reach 2 billion kilograms by 2025, with an average volume per person of 0.8 kilograms in 2023.

The per capita consumption varies widely across the region, depending on the culture and preferences of each country. According to Statista, Japan had the highest per capita consumption in

2016, with 3.3 kilograms per person. South Korea ranked second, with 2.8 kilograms per person. Other countries with high per capita consumption were Taiwan (2.6 kilograms), Vietnam (1.5 kilograms) and Indonesia (1.4 kilograms). In 2023, the revenue in the coffee segment in Asia and the Far East is expected to amount to US$83 billion, with an annual growth rate of 5.17% for 2023-2025. China is the largest market, with projected revenue of US$28.6 billion in 2023. Concerning total population figures, projections indicate per capita revenues of US$16.67 in 2023 in Asia and the Far East. By 2025, 85% of spending and 22% of volume consumption in the coffee segment would be attributable to out-of-home consumption (for example, in bars and restaurants).

Brunei Darussalam

Although it is a small country, located on the northern part of Kalimantan Island, bordering with Malaysia and Indonesia, Brunei Darussalam deserves special mention because it was listed by the ICO as 7th in per capita consumption in 2022 - 8 kilos (17.6 lbs) - which has been steadily growing in recent years. Coffee's popularity sees a significant portion of its population of under half a million enjoying various types of beverages, from traditional brews to more modern concoctions. Several coffee shops and cafes have opened up in urban areas, offering specialty coffees, espresso-based drinks, and a range of other options. The younger generation particularly enjoys spending their time at the cafes, contributing to a growing coffee culture.

China

China is a market being watched closely by the coffee world, viewed as the biggest and fastest-growing market in Asia. The onset of consumption in China dates back to the late 1980s, with steady growth thanks to the promotions of companies such as Starbucks Coffee Company and Nestlé SA. Other significant players are Luigi Lavazza SPA, Gloria Jeans, and JAB Holding Company. Coffee's association with modern trends and fashion has endeared it among the middle class. While the more conservative hold on to their tea culture, there has been staggering growth in coffee consumption, particularly among the younger generations — young professionals and students. Significantly higher coffee consumption is recorded mainly in the urban areas of Shanghai, Beijing and Chengdu. Market intelligence showed that from analysis of 2020 data, one new coffee shop was opened daily in China's Chengdu City, pushing the city's total number of coffee shops to over 4,000, just after Shanghai and Beijing.

Over the last two decades, China has broken rank as a predominantly tea-consumption culture to the acceptance of coffee as an alternative beverage, posting a 30% annual growth rate in consumption, albeit recently cooling down to about 15%. Amazingly, in the 14 years to 2023, consumption in China skyrocketed by more than 1,000%. The China Coffee Association Beijing (CCAB) currently reports an annual growth rate of Chinese consumption of 15% . The opportunities presented by the growing market have significant challenges for foreign companies interested in tapping into it, and one of the best approaches is through partnerships with Chinese entities. Unsurprisingly April 2020 the announcement of a joint venture between Lavazza Group and Yum China Holdings presented great promise for Lavazza. While Lavazza had been in the Chinese market for a while, the company recognised that the Chinese identity in the partnership would significantly enhance its prospects. The joint venture's purpose was to explore the Lavazza coffee shop concept in China, and the opening of a new Lavazza flagship store in Shanghai marked the project's inauguration. On the other hand, Nestlé's recognition of local culture and preferences indicates the identification of consumer sovereignty despite being the market leader. Consequently, Nestle's Sense Cafe released, in May 2020, three new coffee products with unique Yunnan flavours.

Compared to the US and Europe, China's per capita consumption is still meagre, ranging from 5 to 7 cups per year. However, the vast population (just over 1.4 billion in 2023) and its increasing affluence make the Chinese market significant to producers and investors. In September 2023, the global media was awash with the news of Starbucks' opening of a $220 million coffee production and distribution facility in China, which also signalled the company's ambitious plans of expanding its retail footprint in the Chinese market. China's prospects are significant, given that the global rate of consumption growth, as reported by the ICO, is around two per cent, yet China's reported rate is 15%. Additionally, Chinese consumption, especially for younger generations, is observed to be more about status than taste. With the influences of companies such as Starbucks and others that set trends for consumer products, young Chinese professionals tend to craft their identities around Western products. Instant coffee is the most consumed and most popular for home consumption among professionals and students, with the most popular form being the three-in-one, where the coffee is pre-mixed with creamer and sweetener or flavouring.

Japan

Japan is one of the biggest markets in Southeast Asia. The ICO ranks it as the fifth biggest importer of coffee and coffee products globally, and Japan has recognition among the exporters as the Asian anchor in what is known as the traditional coffee market.

A survey in July 2022 indicated that most respondents reported daily coffee consumption and only 10% stated that they never drank coffee. The survey showed that just over one in three people consumed the beverage twice to thrice daily. Most consumption is at home; out of home (café, restaurant and others) is not as strong. Moreover, there has been an increase in soluble or instant coffee consumption which, for some consumers, is much easier and more convenient to prepare at home.

Records show that the Japanese market accounted for almost 433 million tons of coffee in 2021. By the turn of the century, Japan consumed less than 400 million tons. However, over the two decades of the 21st century, an increase of 33 million tons was registered as additional consumption. There has been a noticeable increase in Japanese demand, driven by changes in consumer preferences from tea to coffee. Various studies in Japan have highlighted the health benefits of coffee consumption. The promotion of coffee consumption has been spearheaded by the All Japan Coffee Association (AJCA) over several decades and more recently joined by the Specialty Coffee Association of Japan (SCAJ).

Indonesia

According to the ICO, Indonesia is the fourth biggest producer and exporter of coffee after Brazil, Vietnam and Colombia. However, domestic consumption remained low until recently, as Indonesians historically preferred tea over coffee, but consumption of the latter in Indonesia has grown significantly over the past three decades. Sometime back, the coffee consumption per capita was only 0.8 kg or 800 grams per year, but it grew to around 1.5 kg per year, and the trend is upward.

In 2020, Indonesia consumed 4.8 million 60-kilogram bags, representing 3% of the world total, increasing from 1.3 million bags in 1990 and 3.4 million bags in 2010. Per capita consumption was 1.4 kilograms in 2016, below the global average of 1.6 kilograms, which had increased from 0.5 kilograms in 1990 to 1.1 kilograms in 2010. With an average volume per capita of 0.54 kilograms in 2022, Indonesia's consumption volume was expected to reach 154.8 million kilograms by 2025. Projections by Fitch Solutions show that Indonesia's consumer spending on coffee would grow at an average rate of 8.2%, reaching US$2.2 billion in 2024 from US$1.7 billion in 2020. The consumption growth compares with an expected average increase of 6.5% over the same period for tea.

Consumer preferences in Indonesia have also changed significant, favouring the consumption of fresh coffee in some markets where instant was traditionally consumed. The trend in consumption is reflected in the spread of café culture and the rising popularity of local specialty coffee shops that emphasise local, single-sourced beans and roasting techniques. The 2022 estimates indicated a value of US$2 billion, with an annual growth rate of 5.17 per cent for 2022-2025. Indonesia's largest segment is instant coffee, with a projected market volume of US$1.7 billion in 2022. Considering Indonesia's total population figures, the Indonesian value chain generated revenues of US$7.32 per person in 2022. By 2025, 69% of spending and 14% of volume consumption in the coffee segment will be attributable to out-of-home consumption (for example, in bars and restaurants).

South Korea

South Korea has had a growing coffee market over the last few decades and has been one of the leading growth markets in the world. Coffee is a big deal, though the Korean market seems to be getting saturated. Just like the rest of Asia, South Korea had more than a thousand years of tea culture before coffee entered into that culture to become the most popular drink. According to the Korean Economic Institute of America, South Korea consumes almost 6% of the total Asia-Pacific market. Coffee consumption is a status symbol in South Korea, a powerful class indicator, drinking 12.3 cups per week, thus a per capita consumption of 2.3 kg per year.

South Korea has about 49,000 coffee shops, with an estimated 18,000 in Seoul. In 2022, the Korea Consumer Agency reported that more people frequented coffee shops, revealing that individuals visited cafes an average of 11.7 times per month — more men than women consumed their coffee in a café or restaurant. The innovation of the Dongsuh Foods Corporation with the introduction of instant coffee made consumption convenient to consumers in the 1970s and gave way to the appreciation of brewed coffee. However, it appears that the industry has now reached saturation.

Vietnam

Vietnam is the world's second-largest coffee-producing and exporting country after Brazil. Coffee drinking has become a deep-rooted habit, introduced by the French in the 19th century. Historically, Vietnam has had a tea-drinking culture and has been among the leading global tea producers for a while. However, coffee consumption has started to increase significantly, so Vietnamese consume about 15% of the coffee produced by their country. Coffee drinking has become a deep-rooted habit, especially with the traditional beverage brewed with a special filter and condensed milk. According to Statista, Vietnam consumed approximately 3.1 million 60kg in 2020/21, which increased to approximately 3.2 million 60kg in 2021/2022. Forecasts indicate an increase of 100 thousand bags in 2022/2023. The people in the north (Hanoi) are now drinking more of it, replacing tea with coffee.

India

India is closely associated with tea consumption, but coffee consumption started growing in the middle of the 20th century, soon after India's independence, at an average of 2% per year from 1950 to 2000. However, the 21st century saw a significant increase in India's consumption. Apart from the socio-economic interruption of the COVID-19 pandemic, consumption has grown around 5% yearly since 2001, with projections of an increased rate of around 7.7%.

India

Reports indicate that roughly two in three Indians did not drink coffee in the past, but that has changed; though India's consumption is just under 0.05 kg per capita, demand has increased by 40% in the last decade. With a population of just over 1.42 billion in 2023, when India overtook China as the most populous nation, investors expect to continue exploring the opportunities of tapping into India's coffee consumption prospects. India is one of Nescafe's fastest-growing markets. Two companies, Nestlé and Hindustan Unilever Limited, have a duopoly in supplying packaged coffee of various brands, though Tata Coffee is steadily clawing away at their market share.

Retailers in India respond to customer needs by providing roasted coffee on demand — where a quick take-out roast is done for the customer — also serving creamy beverages for those who want hot coffee. Coffee with milk is dominant in India, perhaps due to the abundance of milk, the country being one of the largest milk producers in Asia. India does not import coffee for consumption; what is imported is only for re-export, since import duty is 100%

for any coffee imported for domestic consumption. Nonetheless, sometimes even with this duty, instant coffee manufacturers import inferior produce as it is cheaper than what is available in India.

Consumption in Oceania

According to the ICO, the consumption in Oceania (which includes Australia, New Zealand, Papua New Guinea and other Pacific islands) was 36.5 million 60-kg bags in the 2020/21 coffee year, an increase of 1.5% from the previous year. The per capita consumption in Oceania was 3.4 kg in 2019, which was higher than the world average of 2.2 kg. Australia accounted for most of the consumption, followed by New Zealand, which consumed 0.9 million 60kg bags of coffee in 2020/21.

Australia, with a population of 26 million, is an important market. According to *Accumulate*, 75% of people report daily consumption. Given the total population, the proportion of coffee consumers is quite significant. The market's revenue was 6.1 billion US dollars in 2022. The most popular choice in cafés and coffee bars was a latte, which cost an average of 4.16 Australian dollars in 2019. Australia imported over 2.1 million 60kg bags in the 2022 financial year, mainly from Brazil, Colombia, and Indonesia.

Coffee consumption is a significant part of the country's culture and lifestyle. Australians take pride in their quality and preparation, with a thriving café culture, particularly in cities like Melbourne, Sydney, and Brisbane. Cafés are popular social spaces where people gather to enjoy coffee, brunch, and socialise. Australian cafés often have a relaxed and welcoming atmosphere, with typical outdoor seating. Australians have a preference for espresso-based coffee. Long black, flat white, cappuccino, and latte are popular choices. Flat white, a coffee beverage that originated in Australia, has gained popularity worldwide. Typically, these drinks are made with one or two shots of espresso and steamed milk. Australians have a high demand for takeaway coffee. "Grab and go" coffee is popular among busy city dwellers who prefer a quick caffeine fix while on the move. Coffee shops offer convenient takeaway options, often using reusable cups or promoting sustainability initiatives.

Australia has embraced the specialty coffee movement, strongly focusing on high-quality beans, ethical sourcing, and expert roasting techniques. Independent specialty coffee shops and micro-roasters have gained popularity, offering a wide range of single-origin and unique blends to cater to connoisseurs. Australians value the quality and texture of milk used in coffee. Baristas pay attention to properly texturizing milk for a smooth and velvety mouthfeel. Dairy alternatives, such as soy, almond, and oat, are also widely available to cater to varying dietary preferences. Many Australians enjoy brewing at home, where espresso machines, capsule systems, and manual brewing methods like French press and pour-over are commonly used. Home brewing allows individuals to experiment with different beans, flavours, and brewing techniques.

The Australian coffee scene features numerous artisanal coffee roasters who roast their beans in-house. They are dedicated to sourcing beans worldwide, often focusing on sustainable and direct trade practices. Their emphasis on craftsmanship and attention to flavour profiles contribute to the country's diverse coffee offerings. Australian enthusiasts have embraced the concept of the "third wave" of coffee, which emphasises the traceability of coffee, craftsmanship, and unique flavour profiles. This movement has increased interest in alternative brewing methods like pour-over, AeroPress, and cold brew.

Australia hosts various coffee events and competitions, such as the Melbourne International Coffee Expo (MICE) and the Australian Specialty Coffee Association (ASCA) competitions. These events showcase the country's coffee talent, facilitate networking among industry professionals, and educate the public about coffee appreciation.

New Zealand is not a big coffee market, given a small population of about five million, but it has a vibrant café culture. According to the Helgi Library, consumption per capita was 4.16 kg in 2020, slightly lower than the peak of 4.28 kg in 2015. Euromonitor says the revenue was US$1.06 billion in 2023, with annual market growth expectations of 5.14% from 2023 to 2025. The most popular was fresh ground coffee pods, which accounted for 42% of retail volume sales in 2020, but many consumers prefer to drink coffee out-of-home rather than at home. Nonetheless, many New Zealanders enjoy brewing at home, using espresso machines, filter coffee makers, and manual brewing methods like French press and pour-over. Home brewing allows individuals to explore different beans, flavours, and brewing techniques.

Coffee consumption in New Zealand is deeply ingrained in the country's culture, and the nation has developed a strong coffee scene known for its quality and innovation, mainly in the cities of Auckland, Wellington, and Christchurch. Cafés and coffee shops are integral to the country's social fabric, serving as meeting places for friends, colleagues, and families. New Zealanders have a preference for espresso-based coffee. Flat whites, cappuccinos, lattes, and long blacks are commonly consumed. Flat white, which originated in Australia but gained popularity in New Zealand, is a signature coffee choice with a strong espresso shot topped with velvety textured milk.

The global specialty coffee movement has also caught on in New Zealand, which has embraced the specialty movement and is home to numerous specialty roasters and independent coffee shops. These establishments often focus on sourcing high-quality beans through direct trade relationships and emphasise artisanal roasting and brewing techniques. They offer a wide range of single-origin and unique coffee blends. New Zealand is known for its artisanal roasters, who roast small batches of beans with care and expertise, prioritising flavour and quality, often experimenting with different profiles and roasting methods. Their passion for craftsmanship has contributed to the country's diverse and thriving coffee scene.

New Zealanders value the quality of the milk used in coffee. Baristas pay attention to properly textured milk, aiming for a smooth and creamy consistency. Dairy alternatives, such as soy, almond, and oat, are widely available to cater to different dietary preferences. Alongside espresso-based coffee, New Zealanders are open to alternative brewing methods. Pour-over, AeroPress, and cold brew have gained popularity, showcasing the country's appreciation for coffee experimentation and different flavour profiles. Like in Australia, takeaway coffee is popular in New Zealand, catering to people's busy lifestyles. Many coffee shops offer convenient takeaway options, allowing customers to enjoy their coffee on the go. Reusable cups are encouraged to promote sustainability and reduce single-use waste.

New Zealand hosts various coffee competitions and events,

including the New Zealand Coffee Festival held in Auckland during March every year, the New Zealand Specialty Coffee Association (NZSCA) Championships, and the New Zealand Barista Championship. These events celebrate the country's coffee talent, foster industry networking, and provide opportunities for coffee education.

Consumption in the Middle East and North Africa

Coffee consumption in the Middle East has a long and rich history and unique cultural significance. It is growing, and the market presents significant opportunities for untapped potential. The Middle East has historically connected with coffee since its discovery in Ethiopia, particularly in the Arabian Peninsula, especially Yemen. *(See more extensive coverage of the Ethiopian coffee ceremony and other coffee cultures in Chapter Six.)*

Coffee has long been a part of Middle Eastern culture, and owing to a significant Arab influence, this culture spread out into North Africa. The Middle East and Gulf region, with Dubai as the business hub, has a market of between 4.5 and 5 million 60-kilogram bags. Consumption habits vary among countries and sub-regions. However, coffee is deeply rooted in tradition, hospitality, and social customs, blending traditional preparations and the growing influence of modern coffee culture.

Dubai is the regional trendsetter and has long been at the centre of new developments in the Middle Eastern market. However, regarding per capita consumption, Lebanon, Algeria, and Qatar top the list. Several chains have opened up in the Middle East in the decade since the debut of Starbucks in 1999, with a significant presence in the UAE and Saudi Arabia. Starbucks alone touts nearly 600 stores in 12 Middle Eastern and North African countries, and employs over 10,000 people. There has been significant growth of chains, independent cafés, and coffee shops, with great potential for further expansion as innovations come in, given the global entrepreneurial explosion in meeting consumer desires.

Traditional coffee preparations such as Turkish coffee and Arabic coffee (also known as *Ghawa or Qahwa)*, are the hallmark of Middle Eastern countries. These coffees are typically strong, dark, and brewed using special methods and pots. They are often served in small cups and accompanied by dates or other sweets. Coffee holds a significant role in Middle Eastern social gatherings and hospitality. Serving coffee is considered a gesture of warmth and hospitality, with guests welcomed with a cup of coffee, and the host continuing to offer refills as a sign of respect and friendship. Middle Eastern coffee is often flavoured with cardamom and other spices like saffron, cloves, or cinnamon. These spices add a distinct aroma and flavour, creating a unique sensory experience.

Coffeehouses, known as *qahwa* or *ahwa* (in Egyptian Arabic), are prominent in Middle Eastern culture. The *ahwa,* or outdoor cafe, is fundamental to Egyptian culture, where one sits outdoors, talking to friends, and doing it all with a delicious coffee. The word "ahwa" is both the name for coffee and the place where one drinks it. These establishments serve as social hubs where people gather for a cup, engage in discussions, play board games, or simply relax. Coffeehouses have historically been important centres for intellectual and cultural exchange. Traditional Middle Eastern coffee is often prepared in a *dallah,* a long-handled coffee pot, and served in small cups called finjans. The *dallah* is made of brass or copper and features a distinctive shape and design. The preparation and serving process itself is considered an art form.

Coffee is often enjoyed alongside dates or other traditional Middle Eastern sweets. The combination of dates and other sweets complements the coffee's flavours and adds a sweet touch to balance its intensity. Middle Eastern countries have embraced the modern coffee culture alongside these traditional preparations. Western-style shops like Starbucks and Costa Coffee have gained popularity in urban areas, offering a variety that includes espresso-based drinks, flavoured coffees, and specialty brews. There is a growing interest in specialty coffee, particularly among younger generations.

Specialty coffee shops, independent roasters, and barista competitions have emerged in several Middle Eastern countries, showcasing a passion for high-quality beans, unique flavour profiles, and advanced brewing techniques. In some countries, a traditional coffee ceremony involves roasting, grinding, and brewing in front of guests. This ceremony adds a cultural and interactive element to the coffee experience, emphasising the importance of hospitality and community.

Saudi Arabia, United Arab Emirates (UAE), Oman, Yemen and Palestine have a traditional coffee ceremony as part of their cultural heritage. In Saudi Arabia it is known as *Ghawa* or *Qahwa*. The coffee is often made with lightly roasted beans and flavoured with cardamom. The host prepares and serves the coffee in small cups called *finjan*. The ceremony symbolises hospitality and is an integral part of social gatherings and events. The UAE also has a *Ghawa,* where the coffee is typically made from dark roasted Arabica beans and flavoured with cardamom. It is brewed in a *dallah*, a long-spouted coffee pot, and served in small cups. Dates or sweets often accompany *Ghawa*.

In Oman, the traditional coffee ceremony is called *Kahwa*, and it involves the use of lightly roasted coffee beans and the addition of cardamom and sometimes other spices. *Kahwa* is brewed in a *dallah* and served in small cups. The coffee ceremony symbolises hospitality and is often accompanied by Omani dates.

Yemen has a long history with coffee; the traditional coffee ceremony is an important part of Yemeni culture. The coffee, known as *qishr* or *bunni*, is made from lightly roasted coffee beans mixed with spices like cardamom, ginger, and cloves. The coffee is brewed in a traditional pot called *majlis* and served in small cups.

In Palestine, the traditional coffee ceremony is known as *jabena*. Palestinian coffee is typically prepared using medium to dark roasted beans and is flavoured with cardamom. The beverage is brewed in a special *jabena* pot and served in small cups. The ceremony often involves roasting the beans and grinding them before brewing.

Coffee consumption in North Africa, particularly in Egypt, Algeria, Morocco, Libya, and Tunisia, is influenced by a rich cultural heritage and historical traditions. Algeria is the leading coffee importer in Africa, with a little over two million bags per year. According to CABI, a UK-based agribusiness research organisation, the main coffee-consuming countries in North Africa are Algeria, Morocco, and Egypt, with per capita consumption of 0.6 kg in Algeria, 0.5 kg in Morocco, and 0.2 kg in Egypt in 2019. North Africa has a strong tradition of brewing and serving Arabic coffee, which is referred to as *qahwa* or *kahwa* in Arabic.

It is typically prepared by roasting coffee beans, grinding them finely, and brewing them in a *dallah* or *ibrik*. It is often flavoured with spices like cardamom, served in small cups, and often consumed as part of social gatherings and hospitality customs. Traditional coffee preparation methods, such as the Moroccan *briq* or the Tunisian *jabana*, involve intricate rituals and have been passed down through the generations.

In North Africa, coffee is commonly enjoyed with sugar, and it is not uncommon to find sweetened or spiced preparations. For example, Moroccan coffee is often sweetened with sugar and flavoured with ingredients like cinnamon or orange blossom water. Algerian and Tunisian coffee preparations may also include a touch of sweetness and various spices. North African cities have a vibrant café culture, with coffee shops serving as social hubs where people gather to relax, socialise, and discuss various topics. These cafés offer many options, including traditional Arabic coffee as well as Western-style espresso-based beverages.

In recent years, North Africa has seen the emergence of specialty coffee shops and an increased interest in specialty coffee. These establishments focus on sourcing high-quality beans, offering different brewing methods, and highlighting coffee's unique flavours and characteristics. However, consumption habits are not uniform between countries and regions.

Consumption in Africa

Consumption in Africa is fascinating because most of the coffee produced in Africa is exported mainly to Europe in its raw form and then imported into Africa — some of it still in raw form and some as a finished product ready for consumption. About half of the African countries are coffee producers, while the other half are consumers. According to the International Coffee Organization, coffee is a primary source of income for more than 12 million households in Africa, particularly for rural-based populations. However, domestic consumption is relatively low compared to other producing regions, accounting for only 4% of global coffee consumption in 2019/20. Ethiopia, however, has a different story from other African countries because it was recognised as the birthplace of coffee centuries ago and has a historical culture of coffee consumption. More so, the country is the largest producer in Africa and Africa's most significant consumer because it consumes nearly 50% of its production locally, an average of 3 million 60-kilogram bags annually.

South Africa is a vital consuming nation. According to Helgi Library, the consumption per capita was 0.93 kg in 2020, which was slightly lower than the peak of 1.11 kg in 2010. According to Euromonitor, the retail sales in South Africa reached R4.9 billion in 2020, and the market was expected to grow annually by 4% from 2020 to 2025. The most popular type in South Africa is instant coffee, accounting for about 77% of retail volume sales.

South Africa also has its own plantations in KwaZulu Natal and Mpumalanga, producing mainly Arabica beans, albeit in relatively small quantities. Most coffee consumed in South Africa is imported. The country has a growing specialty coffee culture, with many independent roasters and cafés offering high-quality experiences.

African producer countries primarily focus on exporting coffee beans rather than catering to the domestic market. This export-oriented focus has influenced the availability and accessibility of coffee within the countries, except for Ethiopia. Even though there is strong competition between local consumption and export, the country is still using quite a large percentage of its produce without restriction. Although brewing using traditional methods such as the *jebena* pot is prevalent, an emerging café culture led by Kaldi's café is now ubiquitous in the capital, Addis Ababa.

In Eastern, Central and Southern Africa, there is increased awareness and education due to the impact of the African Fine Coffees Association (AFCA), which has chapters in most of these countries, providing training in different aspects of preparation. Consumers in the region's urban areas are becoming more educated about coffee, its origins, and brewing methods. There is a growing interest in learning about different coffee varieties, brewing techniques, and an emerging specialty coffee culture. In partnership with national coffee authorities, AFCA's education programmes, workshops, and barista training initiatives have increased knowledge among consumers. While coffee shops and cafes thrive in urban areas, on-the-go consumption is also growing — with takeaway coffee options, such as grab-and-go stands or mobile carts — which cater to busy urban lifestyles and provide convenient access to coffee for professionals and commuters. Overall, the Eastern African urban areas are experiencing a dynamic consumption trend, characterised by a growing café culture, a shift towards specialty coffee, an emphasis on high-quality, increased consumer awareness, and a blend of sit-in and on-the-go options. This has been so true in Kenya, Rwanda, Tanzania and Uganda, where the proliferation of cafés is easily noticeable everywhere. Coffee is also often consumed locally in homes, workplaces, and social gatherings.

In Kenya's urban areas, coffee consumption has been experiencing a notable trend in recent years, particularly in cities like Nairobi and Mombasa, which have witnessed the emergence of a vibrant café culture. There is a noticeable shift towards specialty coffee in Kenya's urban areas. Specialty coffee refers to high-quality coffee that is meticulously grown, harvested, and processed to highlight unique flavours and characteristics. This is attributed to the significant impact of the barista training promoted by AFCA over two decades. Enthusiasts and a younger generation of consumers are increasingly seeking out specialty experiences, leading to the rise of specialty coffee shops.

Rwanda, a member of the East Africa Community, has made significant strides in the specialty sector, both in production and consumption. Consumption is increasing, and the country has seen the establishment of coffee shops and cafés that serve Rwandan specialty coffee. The emergence of coffee shops and cafes in major cities like Kigali has contributed to the growing coffee consumption trend. These establishments serve a variety of beverages, including espresso-based drinks, pour-over brews, and traditional Rwandan coffee preparations. The government has proactively promoted the domestic industry and encouraged local consumption, with initiatives launched to educate and raise awareness among Rwandans about the country's high-quality coffee and the benefits of supporting the local sector. Efforts have been made to make export-quality produce accessible to the local market. Consumers have access to premium coffee options that were previously primarily reserved for international markets.

Tanzania has a growing café culture that reflects the country's rich coffee heritage and the increasing appreciation for specialty coffee. As a country known for high-quality produce, Tanzanian cafes often showcase locally grown beans. There is a focus on promoting Tanzanian coffee and its unique flavour profiles, allowing locals and visitors to experience its distinct tastes, given the country's high tourism traffic. These establishments often work closely with local coffee farmers and cooperatives to ensure traceability and quality. They may offer single-origin coffees, specialty brewing methods, and baristas with expertise in creating exceptional experiences. While specialty coffee is gaining popularity, traditional preparations are still an integral part of the café culture. Tanzanian coffee rituals, such as brewing coffee with a *dallah* (traditional coffee pot) or serving spiced coffee, continue to be practised in households and certain establishments. These traditional methods highlight the cultural significance of the beverage in Tanzanian society. Local cafes serve as social spaces and gathering spots for nationals and visitors alike. They provide a place to relax, meet friends, conduct business meetings, or simply enjoy a cup of coffee. The atmosphere in local cafes is often laid-back, fostering a sense of community and encouraging conversations over a cup.

The café culture is evolving, with an increasing focus on specialty coffee, traditional preparations, and a commitment to promoting the national brand. Whether enjoying a cup of coffee in a specialty café, participating in traditional rituals, or engaging in conversations with fellow coffee lovers, the café culture of Tanzania offers a delightful experience for enthusiasts and those seeking to explore the country's coffee heritage. There is increasing domestic consumption, with Dar es Salaam, the largest city, having a growing café scene with several notable establishments that cater to enthusiasts and provide unique coffee experiences, which include Africafe Café, Cape Town Fish Market Café, Tanzibar Coffee House, Fix Café, and the Village Museum Café.

Africafe Café is a well-known café chain with multiple branches across Dar es Salaam. They serve a variety of coffee drinks made from Tanzanian-grown beans. Africafe offers a comfortable and casual setting for coffee lovers to relax and enjoy their beverages. Other cafés include the Cape Town Fish Market Café, a popular café located in the Slipway area of Dar es Salaam, which offers a range of coffee options, including espresso-based drinks and specialty coffees. Tanzibar Coffee House is a charming café in Dar es Salaam's heart. They specialise in Tanzanian coffee, offering a variety of single-origin and blended coffee drinks. At the same time, Fix Café is a trendy café located in the Mikocheni area of Dar es Salaam, offering a range of coffee options. It is known for its high-quality beans sourced from various regions and its commitment to promoting Tanzanian coffee culture. Village Museum Café is situated within the Village Museum, offering visitors a unique coffee experience. The café provides a serene setting surrounded by traditional Tanzanian huts and exhibits, where guests can enjoy locally sourced coffee while immersing themselves in the country's cultural heritage. Noticeably, the city continues to witness the emergence of new coffee shops and specialty cafes, with each café having its own distinct ambience, coffee offerings, and menu options, contributing to the diverse coffee culture.

Uganda, Africa's leading exporter, which hitherto did not consume much coffee, has a new café culture leading to a transformation, focusing on specialty coffee, education, and the creation of inviting spaces. As consumption increases globally, Uganda has also seen a rise in local consumption. Ugandans are increasingly embracing the beverage as a part of their daily routine, at home and in cafes. It is enjoyed in various forms, including traditional methods like boiling or brewing with a cloth filter and modern espresso-based drinks. The growth of the café industry and increased consumption have had a positive economic impact on the country. The rise in domestic consumption creates new market opportunities, stimulates local production, and supports the livelihoods of smallholder coffee farmers.

The increase in consumption, both domestically and in cafes, reflects the growing appreciation for Ugandan coffee and the evolving tastes and preferences of Ugandan consumers. Uganda has seen a surge in specialty coffee shops and cafes that focus on providing high-quality experiences. These establishments source and roast their own beans, often highlighting locally-grown ones. Specialty cafes offer a variety of brewing methods, including pour-over, espresso-based drinks, and alternative brewing techniques, catering to discerning enthusiasts.

Urban areas, particularly Kampala, have witnessed the development of a vibrant café culture, which are popular social spaces for locals and expatriates, providing an atmosphere for relaxation, work, or socialising. The café scene offers diverse experiences, from cosy neighbourhood coffee shops to trendy and modern establishments. With the rise of specialty cafes, there has been an increased focus on coffee education and consumer awareness. Cafés often engage in cupping sessions, brewing workshops, and barista training to educate customers about different Ugandan coffee origins, flavour profiles, and brewing techniques.

Ugandans are very social people, and Kampala, the capital city, has a growing café scene with several significant establishments that cater to enthusiasts and provide unique coffee experiences. Café Javas is a well-known café chain with several branches across the city. They serve a wide range of coffee-based beverages, including espresso, blended, and single-origin coffees. Café Javas is also known for its diverse food menu and spacious, comfortable seating areas. Endiro Coffee is a popular café chain with multiple locations. They focus on ethically sourced, Ugandan-grown coffee beans and offer a variety of specialty drinks. Endiro is known for its vibrant atmosphere, quality coffee, and commitment to social impact. Other cafes include the Caramel Café, Coffee & Cake, Prunes Café and Bakery, 1000 Cups Coffee House, and Kardamom & Koffee. There are many more emerging coffee shops and specialty cafés worth exploring in the capital city and other cities. Each offers its own distinctive atmosphere, coffee selection, and menu options, contributing to a vibrant coffee culture.

In Central Africa, the consumption of coffee in Cameroon and the Democratic Republic of the Congo (DRC) is relatively moderate. Coffee is an important export crop, but various factors influence domestic consumption, including the historical orientation of coffee being for export and not for local consumption. Coffee is commonly consumed in households, often prepared using traditional methods such as brewing with a cloth filter or a simple drip system. However, other beverages like tea and cocoa are also popular.

In some regions of Cameroon, coffee consumption is associated with social gatherings, hospitality, and traditional ceremonies, where it may be served to guests as a gesture of welcome. However, the cultural preference for other beverages and economic factors as well, play a role in the overall consumption levels. In recent years, there has been a growing interest in specialty coffee in Cameroon. In partnership with AFCA, some producers and entrepreneurs are exploring the potential of specialty coffee, including single-origin and specialty-grade beans. Specialty shops and cafes are beginning to emerge in urban areas, particularly in major cities like Yaoundé and Douala.

Promotion of local consumption is championed through Festicoffee. Initiated by the Cocoa and Coffee Inter-professional Council of Cameroon (CICC), Festicoffee is a festival that promotes and celebrates the richness of coffee produced locally, while also seeking to improve revenue and the living standards of producers in Cameroon. Through the festival and other engagements, coordinated initiatives by government entities, cooperatives, and industry stakeholders are increasing awareness and appreciation of locally produced coffee. These efforts seek to grow domestic consumption and establish a coffee culture.

The Democratic Republic of the Congo (DRC) has faced challenges due to conflict and instability. However, coffee consumption remains significant, especially in big urban centres and other traditional coffee-consuming communities, such as Ubangi (in North-Western DRC). Even in rural markets, roast and ground coffee is available and customers buy it the same way they buy other food products in the open-air market, and is consumed often in households. There is a preference for stronger, darker roasts and intense flavours. The flavour profile of the coffee consumed within the country is often adapted to local tastes. Various factors, including historical challenges and recent developments, have influenced consumption.

In spite of the challenges, including poor infrastructure, the specialty coffee sector in the DRC has evolved thanks to AFCA in partnership with Congolese coffee companies, cooperatives, Café Africa RDC and the coffee regulation body (ONAPAC: Office des Produits Agricoles du Congo), which has led to improvement of quality. There is a growing recognition of the potential of the DRC's coffee industry, both domestically and internationally. There is a growing number of locally produced, roasted and packaged coffee and a number of brands such as Café Kivu and

Virunga Origins are getting to the international market. Congo Robusta has been traditionally appreciated by the Southern Italian market, where it has the reputation of producing good "spuma" when used in espresso blends. It is interesting to see roasters such as Everybody's Coffee, in Chicago, who have successfully introduced Karawa Robusta Coffee from the Ubangi Region to American consumers, and is being well appreciated by the Gen-Z, taken espresso-based, cold brew, or nitro. The awareness drive has led to a gradual increase in domestic coffee consumption. The trend is still developing, and various factors, such as infrastructure improvements, market access, and economic stability, will shape future consumption patterns.

Nigeria, Ghana, Senegal and Ivory Coast are the significant coffee consumers in West Africa. Nigeria has a large population with the greatest potential for a significant increase in consumption beyond what is currently known as instant coffee, which is popular due to its convenience and affordability. However, there is also a growing interest in specialty coffee, and specialty shops are emerging in urban areas.

In Ivory Coast (Côte d'Ivoire), the world's largest producer of cocoa and one of Africa's key coffee producers, coffee consumption has historically been low. However, there are ongoing efforts to promote consumption and a developing specialty coffee scene. Over the ten years to 2023 there has been a progressive emergence of cafés in Abidjan, and a developing coffee consumption culture in different parts of the country.

In Ghana, coffee consumption is growing, but it is not as deeply ingrained in the culture compared to other beverages like tea or cocoa. Nevertheless, in its limited form, local coffee consumption also often involves traditional brewing methods, such as using a cloth filter or a simple drip system. Coffee is often consumed in urban areas and among the middle class, with a focus on instant and instant mixes. There is an emerging interest in specialty coffee, and specialty shops can be found in major cities. There is a growing love for the beverage and a proliferation of cafés in Accra and other cities hints at a new trend.

In Senegal, coffee consumption is deeply rooted in the culture. Traditional preparation methods, such as brewing with spices like cloves and served in a small cup called a *tasse*, are still practised. Coffee is often prepared in households and is a part of daily life and social interactions. A unique aspect of consumption in Senegal is "Café Touba," a spiced coffee named after the holy city of Touba. Café Touba is prepared by mixing coffee with Guinea pepper (grains of paradise) and sometimes other spices like cloves or cinnamon. It has a distinct flavour and is often associated with religious ceremonies and events. Instant coffee is widely consumed due to its convenience and affordability. However, there is also a growing café culture, particularly in urban areas like Dakar. Coffee shops and cafés offer various options, including traditional preparations and modern espresso-based beverages.

With increasing urbanisation in Africa and a growing middle class, café-culture is increasingly becoming a significant phenomenon in cities. Nigeria, though a coffee-producing country, imports coffee to meet the demand of its emerging café business. Sadly, though, most coffee producers have not tasted their coffee as the crop was traditionally grown for export – to earn foreign exchange. This must be considered an opportunity to develop consumption in the local rural coffee-producing areas of African countries and among producers who usually have never tasted their own wares. The Inter-African Coffee Organisation (IACO) launched a campaign to promote domestic consumption in producer countries. Nigeria is a key target, owing to its enormous potential, given a population of 212 million. In 2019, the African Union launched the African Continental Free Trade Area (AfCFTA), now viewed by African producers as an opportunity to promote the transformation of the African coffee value chain to take advantage of the business opportunities across the vast continent.

Conclusion

For a long time, the traditional markets of Europe and North America were the anchors of global coffee consumption. However, emerging markets are growing, showing new preferences, with increasing consumption as new coffee cultures evolve. Promotion capitalises on local tastes, preferences and cultural norms. The growth in emerging markets could be augmented by significantly high populations, improving economic conditions and disposable incomes that translate into higher effective demand. The traditional markets might soon become different reference points rather than what we have always known about them. Innovations and technological enhancements have made soluble coffee more attractive to consumers in emerging markets. There is a revolution in the consumption market because of significant improvements in instant coffee. Estimates indicate that instant coffee corresponds to nearly 25% of total global consumption, with a growth of 2.5 to 3% per year, higher than roasted coffee, and that the beverage indeed has health benefits which consumers need to be educated about. The next chapter discusses coffee and health, and highlights some studies that provide helpful information to guide consumption habits.

3

Overview of Coffee and Health

I remember a great gentleman in the coffee sector, Dr Ernesto Illy, who though no longer with us, made an outstanding contribution to the global industry. During ICO meetings, his voice was always resolute when presenting scientific facts and evidence to counter negative stories about coffee. The good news is that coffee's case is stronger now than ever. Numerous independent studies in different markets indicate how one gets more from their coffee beverage than ever thought. Being a chemist, Dr Illy spoke with authority, quoting several studies that gave a long list of chemical substances in coffee that can help guard against certain conditions, including Alzheimer's disease, heart disease and colon health issues. Coffee has over 100 different substances that interact with the human body in different ways. To most people, the first thing that comes to mind when they think about coffee is caffeine. However, nutrition experts advise that coffee also contains antioxidants and a host of active substances that can reduce internal inflammation and protect against disease.

Coffee and Health Benefits

Coffee has been the subject of numerous studies examining its potential effects on health. It has antioxidant properties, provides energy and mental alertness, enhances physical performance, enhances metabolism, improves liver health, boosts mental health, positively affects cardiovascular health, and generally has protective effects. It is a rich source of antioxidants such as chlorogenic acids and polyphenols, which have been associated with various health benefits. Antioxidants help protect the body against oxidative stress and reduce the risk of chronic diseases. One of the most well-known effects is coffee's ability to increase energy levels and promote mental alertness, primarily due to caffeine, a natural stimulant. Moderate caffeine consumption can enhance cognitive function, improve concentration, and reduce fatigue. Caffeine has also been shown to enhance physical performance, improving endurance, increasing muscle strength and power, and reducing perceived exertion during exercise. Its effect on endurance explains why caffeine is a common ingredient in many sports and performance-enhancing supplements. However, some reports give a negative opinion of the relationship between coffee and health, which some researchers objectively debunk.

The potential health benefits of drinking coffee include protection against Type-2 diabetes, Parkinson's disease, liver disease, and liver cancer. It would, of course, be wise for a person with specific health issues to seek a doctor's advice when deciding how much coffee to consume. One study published in 2007, carried out by Hyon Choi and others over 12 years, involving over 45,000 men, looked at coffee consumption and the risk of incident gout in men and concluded that long-term consumption showed a lower risk of gout. Other studies have also reported that coffee consumption may support cardiovascular health. In the 1990s, the ICO started a series on coffee and health, publishing articles on different aspects, showing research from various scientists on the effects of coffee on human health. Those studies revealed many exciting findings indicating numerous benefits to human health.

Coffee consumption is associated with several metabolic benefits. It may help boost metabolism, increase fat oxidation, and improve insulin sensitivity. Some studies have suggested that regular coffee consumption is associated with a lower risk of type 2 diabetes. Moderate consumption has been linked to a reduced risk of liver diseases, including liver cirrhosis, liver fibrosis, and hepatocellular carcinoma. Coffee's protective effects on the liver may be attributed to its ability to reduce inflammation and oxidative stress in the liver. The relationship between coffee consumption and cardiovascular health is complex and still debated. Moderate consumption is generally considered safe for most people.

Caffeine may stimulate the release of certain neurotransmitters in the brain, such as dopamine and serotonin, which can positively impact mood. Thus, coffee consumption has been associated with a lower risk of depression and a reduced risk of suicide. Some studies suggest that regular coffee consumption may have a protective effect against certain conditions, such as Parkinson's disease, Alzheimer's disease, and certain types of cancer (for example, liver, colorectal, and endometrial cancer). However, more research is needed to understand these relationships better. Health experts have warned that individual responses to coffee can vary, and excessive consumption or sensitivity to caffeine may lead to negative effects such as insomnia, jitteriness, or increased heart rate. Additionally, the addition of sugar, cream, or flavourings to coffee can impact its overall healthfulness. Experts, therefore, advise consumption in moderation as part of a balanced and varied diet, and individuals with specific health conditions should consult their healthcare provider for personalised advice.

Need for Reference to Scientific Studies

Some studies have found that coffee consumption gives one a longer life by lowering chances of death from some causes that lead to coronary heart disease, stroke, diabetes and kidney disease. For instance, some substances in coffee enhance the body's ability to process glucose (or sugar). Thus some of the theories behind the studies found that regular coffee drinkers were less likely to get type-2 diabetes. Studies also noted that regular coffee drinkers were less likely to develop heart failure. Some dieticians recommend drinking one to two cups of coffee daily to ward off heart failure in some cases where the heart has weakened and has complications in pumping blood around the body.

As already noted, some studies have concluded that regular coffee drinkers are less likely to develop Parkinson's disease, because of the caffeine content, which was also found to be helpful in improving control of movement for those with the condition. Studies have also shown improved liver health for regular coffee drinkers, which applies to both regular and decaffeinated coffee, as observations in the consumption of both types seemed to provide a protective effect on the liver. The analysis from the research concluded that coffee drinkers were more likely to have levels of liver enzymes within a healthy range than people who did not drink coffee.

Some studies have also reported that coffee strengthens DNA. Those studies found that dark roast coffee decreases breakage in DNA strands — a phenomenon naturally occurring and linked to the onset of cancer or tumours if not repaired by the body's cells. Other studies showed that coffee drinkers reduced the odds of colon cancer, and researchers found that consumers of both decaf and regular coffee, were 26 per cent less likely to develop colorectal cancer. In the United States, trends have shown that women make up almost two-thirds of Americans living with Alzheimer's disease — and from studies that have been conducted, caffeine was found to offer protection against developing the condition, where two cups could provide a significant advantage. In the case of women aged 65 and older who drank two to three cups daily, the researchers found that these were generally less likely to develop dementia. It was also found that daily drinking of at least one cup of coffee lowers stroke risk, particularly for women.

For pregnant or breastfeeding mothers, doctors give different advice, thus it is imperative for one to consult their obstetrician before adding caffeine to their diet. Where coffee gives one the jitters, it is advisable not to overdo it because caffeine tolerance varies from person to person. One could still get some health benefits by having one cup a day, or even decaf. What one adds to their cup, for instance sugar or milk, can make a difference in how healthful the beverage is. The use of milk substitutes (such as milk from soy, almonds, oats and other non-dairy sources) plus naturally sweet spices and flavourings can be beneficial in place of loading up on cream and sugar. Thus, one could consider stirring a ¼ teaspoon of different flavours such as vanilla extract, cardamom, cinnamon, and cocoa powder. One must also ensure to eat a balanced diet, have regular exercise and maintain a healthy weight so that enjoying coffee becomes a delightful addition in consideration of key health factors. There have been numerous studies on coffee and health, but mention is made of one from Korea, as discussed below.

Example of Korean Studies on Coffee

A study in South Korea noted a rapid increase of colorectal cancer incidence and mortality, possibly related to increased metabolic syndrome among Korean adults between the years 2010 and 2020. The study that also noted that people with metabolic syndrome had a greater risk of developing colorectal cancer, and this was confirmed in both men and women. Meanwhile other studies examined the association between metabolic syndrome and coffee consumption, and showed evidence of an inverse association, which means a potential relationship between higher coffee consumption and a lower risk of developing metabolic syndrome. In scientific terms, metabolic syndrome is a cluster of conditions that increase the risk of cardiovascular disease, type 2 diabetes, and other health issues.

The components of metabolic syndrome typically include abdominal obesity, elevated blood pressure, high blood sugar levels, high triglyceride levels, and low levels of "good" cholesterol (referred to as HDL cholesterol). An inverse association means that as coffee consumption increases, the risk of metabolic syndrome appears to decrease. In other words, individuals who consume more coffee may have a lower likelihood of developing metabolic syndrome compared to those who consume less or none. This is a generalisation and should not be taken to mean that the inverse association necessarily implies causation. While the studies suggest a potential link between coffee consumption and a reduced risk of metabolic syndrome, further research is needed to establish any cause-and-effect relationship and to understand the underlying mechanisms involved.

Additionally, it is crucial to consider other factors that may influence the relationship between coffee consumption and metabolic syndrome. Lifestyle factors, such as diet, physical activity, and overall dietary patterns, can also play a role in the development of metabolic syndrome. Therefore, the inverse association observed in these studies may be influenced by confounding variables not fully accounted for in the analysis of the studies referred to in the above arguments. With the numerous diseases brought about by modern lifestyles, it is crucial to fully understand the potential health benefits of coffee consumption on metabolic syndrome. Individuals who opt to review multiple studies to consider the overall body of evidence would do well to consult healthcare professionals for personalised advice.

Reference to Dietary Guidelines for Americans

The Dietary Guidelines for Americans provide recommendations and advice on various aspects of nutrition, including coffee consumption. The most recent edition of the guidelines is the 2020-2025 edition which states that moderate coffee consumption can be part of a healthy eating pattern. Moderate caffeine intake, including coffee, is generally defined as consuming up to 400 milligrams (mg) of caffeine daily. This amount is equivalent to approximately three to five 8-ounce cups, depending on the coffee's strength and brewing method.

The Guidelines also mention that most healthy individuals can tolerate moderate caffeine intake without adverse effects. However, advice is given for individuals to be aware of their own sensitivity to caffeine and to consider any potential interactions with medications or existing health conditions. Further, the guidelines advise against adding excessive amounts of sugar or high-fat dairy products to coffee, as these additions can contribute to increased calorie and saturated fat intake. Instead, choosing lower-fat or plant-based milk options and using minimal or no added sweeteners is encouraged. Though given to the American population, these guidelines could be useful to people elsewhere. It should be noted that the guidelines may vary for specific populations or individuals with unique health conditions. Thus, it is always advisable, and highly recommended, to consult with a healthcare professional or registered dietitian for personalised advice regarding coffee consumption and overall dietary patterns.

Conclusion

Coffee is a beverage that is enjoyed by many all over the world. However, there are reports of people who become jittery after taking caffeinated drinks with some experiencing an increased heart rate or palpitations, raised blood pressure, anxiety, and trouble falling asleep, which raises the question of how much coffee one should drink and yet avoid adverse effects. In general, there have been extensive studies by various scientific researchers and institutions, with coffee consumption associated with both positive and adverse health effects. Some studies suggest that moderate consumption may have potential benefits, such as increased alertness, improved cognitive function, and a reduced risk of certain diseases like Parkinson's disease and liver disease.

There is a warning that excessive coffee consumption or the addition of unhealthy ingredients like sugar or creamers may adversely affect one's health. Coffee drinkers who experience any adverse effects need to seek the advice of a knowledgeable health professional to guide them on what actions to take. For example, according to the Dietary Guidelines for Americans, drinking three to five cups a day with a maximum intake of 400 milligrams of caffeine is safe. One has to note that caffeine content varies depending on the type of coffee, but an average 8-ounce cup has

95 milligrams, thus the recommendation of a maximum of five cups. The next chapter discusses the issue of coffee and poverty, illustrating the poverty profiles among coffee producers and the call for action to address the challenges.

ABOVE: *A coffee seedling. The management of a coffee nursery is critical in the production of good planting material. (Photo courtesy of UCDA)*

BELOW: *Management of a new coffee garden. (Photo courtesy of NUCAFE)*

ABOVE: *Following recommended procedures in planting coffee. (Photo courtesy of NUCAFE)*

BELOW: *Coffee inter-planted with banana trees. Inter-planting helps with diversification and food security. (Photo courtesy of NUCAFE)*

ABOVE: *A well-mulched coffee garden. Mulching helps to conserve moisture, enhances soil quality and reduces growth of weeds. Decomposed mulch provides organic matter to the soil, improving its fertility. (Photo courtesy of UCDA)*

BELOW: *The farmer must pay attention to coffee trees, inspecting them periodically to ensure freedom from pests and diseases, followed by appropriate action. (Photo courtesy of NUCAFE)*

ABOVE: *Women play a vital role in the coffee industry worldwide. (Photo courtesy of NUCAFE)*

BELOW: *During the harvesting season, women are more diligent in harvesting only the ripe coffee cherries, which ensures quality. A well-rounded cup of coffee is only possible when the harvesting is done right. (Photo courtesy of NUCAFE)*

ABOVE: *Freshly harvested ripe coffee cherries. (Photo courtesy of NUCAFE)*

BELOW: *Well-handled coffee cherries lead to fine-looking processed beans. (Photo courtesy of UCDA)*

ABOVE: *Smallholder farmers tend to have higher operation costs due to their small capacity. Poverty is common, also evidenced in the quality of dressing. (Photo courtesy of NUCAFE)*

BELOW: *Some farmers work together and have processing factories where they can reap economies of scale. (Photo courtesy of NUCAFE)*

ABOVE: *Appropriate equipment helps in the primary and secondary processing of coffee. (Photo courtesy of NUCAFE)*

BELOW: *Sample roasters are used to check the coffee's quality and final grading before export. (Photo courtesy of UCDA)*

ABOVE: *After samples are roasted, a comprehensive cup-tasting process ensures that customer requirements are met. (Photo courtesy of NUCAFE)*

BELOW: *Part of the analysis considers the uniformity of the roasting before the coffee is ground for cup-tasting. (Photo courtesy of UCDA)*

4

Coffee and Poverty

Many people in the West associate coffee with big money because the value chain in developed countries is worth hundreds of billions of dollars. Some well-known coffee business owners in those countries are billionaires. When I was young, in the rural setting of Buganda, in the heart of Uganda, those who cultivated coffee were generally better off than those who did not. Most of my contemporaries have fond memories of how coffee significantly contributed to their educational journey. Our parents made good money from coffee and provided for us in incredible ways. Unfortunately, for present-day coffee producers, this is no longer the case! It appears that today, there is more poverty among coffee farming communities than was the case four to five decades ago. The 2022 UNDP Human Development Report pointed out that 1.2 billion people are multi-dimensionally poor, of whom 579 million live in Sub-Saharan Africa, while 385 million are from South Asia.

The Multidimensional Poverty Index

Global poverty statistics indicate significant poverty in coffee-producing countries. In 2010, Oxford University's Poverty and Human Development Initiative (OPHI), in partnership with United Nations Development Programme (UNDP), developed the global multidimensional poverty index (MPI).

The MPI is described as *"an international measure of acute multidimensional poverty covering over 100 developing countries. It complements traditional monetary poverty measures by simultaneously capturing the acute deprivations in health, education, and living standards that a person faces."* The MPI is a great addition to the traditional measures of monetary poverty. The data analysed in determining the MPI may vary from one country to another. However, it concerns severe deprivations that people concurrently face in health, education, and living standards. When this is applied to coffee farmers, the results have been alarming.

The MPI shows the interlinked aspects of poverty that must be addressed to have a breakthrough in addressing the deprivations faced by the poor. Ethiopia and Uganda, the major African coffee-producing countries, have been mapped to have significantly high poverty indices. Ethiopia, the origin of Arabica coffee and Uganda, the origin of Robusta coffee, face the same plight regarding multidimensional poverty among farmers. The MPI resonates with the Universal Declaration of Human Rights (UDHR) of the United Nations, which gives some guidelines regarding every person's right to a decent living. The UNDR's Article 25 (part 1) states as follows:

Everyone has the right to a standard of living adequate for the health and well-being of himself and of his family, including food, clothing, housing and medical care and necessary social services, and the right to security in the event of unemployment, sickness, disability, widowhood, old age or other lack of livelihood in circumstances beyond his control.

The challenge of poverty is formidable, as observed the poverty situation among coffee farmers. It is imperative to find ways to address this challenge and support efforts to resolve it. In some African countries, there are conflicting actions where some policies seem to entrench poverty among their citizens. However, we hope that the political implications of multidimensional poverty will push the decision-makers to take appropriate action. In his statement at the official opening of the 55th Session of the Economic Commission for Africa (ECA) Conference of African Ministers of Finance, Planning and Economic Development on 16th March 2023, Mr Antonio Pedro, Acting Executive Secretary of the ECA, made an important observation. He stated, "*All in all, 695 million people in Africa are either poor or face the risk of falling into poverty. This represents 50 per cent of the continent's population.*"

We know that Africa has the most countries in coffee production — 25 out of 50 globally in all the coffee-producing regions (that is, Africa, Asia, South, Central and South America). Sadly, lamentations about poverty are a common feature among the coffee-producing communities in all these regions. As an African, I am deeply concerned about poverty and coffee in Africa. Of course, it is incumbent on the African countries' leadership to develop strategies to take their people out of poverty and into a prosperous future. There is a need to transform Africa's coffee sector to address the rampant poverty. Now, the question is, how will this be done? It is a formidable challenge.

Poverty Profiles

A poverty profile is an analysis showing the nature of poverty and its variation across subgroups of society. The profile outlines the significant facts on poverty. In this case, the context is the coffee producer. Although this chapter does not examine how poverty varies among coffee producers by geography, community, livelihoods, and other characteristics, it looks at an analysis of key characteristics of the poor versus non-poor. It examines the reference to a critical asset of a motor vehicle among coffee producers. The 2022 MPI Report noted that poverty reduction at scale is possible. It also divulged new 'poverty profiles' that can offer a breakthrough in development efforts to tackle the interlinked aspects of poverty. There is a series of deprivation bundles that the report identifies as "recurring patterns of poverty," and the poverty profiles have a pattern that tends to be evident in some places. The available data referenced by the MPI indicates that 1.2 billion people, mostly from developing countries, live in conditions that are characteristic of acute multidimensional poverty.

The poverty levels might be linked to the fact that the farmers are smallholders with limited access to essential services, and we could find some patterns among them that point to a vicious cycle of poverty. The farmers need diversified sources of income because their earnings are so small that they cannot cover their needs; consequently somey suffer from malnutrition and poor health. Their children have limited access to good education, and their living standards are deplorable. This pattern is prevalent in most coffee-producing countries. It is important to understand the causes of poverty among coffee producers and to appreciate the plight of farmers. The farmgate price is a vital factor when seeking to understanding the poverty level.

Coffee, the most traded commodity after oil, has its base price determined at the two major global commodity exchanges, one in New York City and the other in London, England, both operating under the Intercontinental Exchange (ICE); thus, we have ICE Futures US and ICE Futures Europe, respectively. Previously, the New York-based exchange was known as the New York Board of Trade (NYBT), and the one in the UK was the London International Financial Futures and Options Exchange (LIFFE). However, the two exchanges were consolidated under ICE after mergers and acquisitions, and they determine the prices of both Robusta and Arabica coffee on a daily basis. The fact that these institutions are detached from the realities of coffee production causes farmers worldwide to detest their influence on price determination for they are viewed as keeping producers poor. This poverty concern is seen in light of the cost of manufactured goods, whose prices rise year-on-year, while coffee prices tend to have a see-saw pattern, generally working against farmer prosperity. The examples that follow illustrate the producers' concerns.

The Cost of a Motor Vehicle in 1980 vs 2023

The Toyota Corolla is a reasonably standard car in most coffee-producing countries. In 1980, a new Toyota Corolla cost just $4,348 in the USA. The manufacturer's recommended retail price for a 2023 Toyota Corolla is $21,550, an average starting price for the compact car class; otherwise, the price would increase to between $23,000 and $24,000. In 1980, the price for Arabica coffee averaged $3.14 per pound (or $6.92 per kg). According to the February 2023 monthly report of the International Coffee Organisation (ICO), the average price for Arabica coffee on the ICE Futures USA was $1.8093 per pound ($3.9887 per kg). For Robusta coffee, the average price in 1980 was about $1.58 per pound ($3.48 per kg), but the average Robusta price for February 2023 on ICE Futures Europe was $0.9426 per pound ($2.07 per kg).

From the above figures, it is evident that coffee producers are worse off in the 2020s than they were in 1980. The average Arabica price was $6.92 per kilo in February 1980, and a farmer would have sold about 630 kilos to buy a Toyota Corolla. In February

2023, the Arabica farmer will have sold their coffee at a price lower than that of 1980, at around $3.99 per kilo and required to sell 5,764 kilos to buy a Toyota Corolla at the 2023 price of $23,000. The Robusta farmer is much worse off than the Arabica farmer and would have to sell almost double the volume of coffee, compared to that of his/her Arabica counterpart, to buy the 2023 Toyota Corolla. The above example attempts to illustrate the poverty status of the farmer who is worse off today compared to 1980, even before adjusting the figures for inflation.

We can also look at another illustration involving a Toyota Land Cruiser. This off-road vehicle is handy for farmers where the infrastructure requires a 4-wheel drive vehicle. Farmers do not need the luxury version but a basic one that can endure the harsh terrain in most coffee-growing regions. The Toyota Land Cruiser of 1980 was a smaller all-terrain off-road vehicle, and in 1980 it would have cost the Arabica farmer about $8,288, for which they would have sold 1.2 tons of coffee at the 1980 average price. In 2023, the Toyota Land Cruiser is around $85,000, which is more than ten times the 1980 price, for which the Arabica farmer would need to sell just over 21 tons of coffee at the 2023 price for coffee. Again, over this four-decade period, the plight of the Robusta coffee farmer worsened off as they would have to sell considerably more coffee to buy the Corolla or the Landcruiser.

Fragile Situation

I remember when I was in high school in the 1970s, and there was a topic of debate that 'African countries are poor because of their dependency on the export of raw materials'. I also recall the discussion on 'banana republics', described as those countries whose economies depended on the export of bananas and were fragile because of the volatility of the price of bananas. On the other hand, coffee is a commodity that has been the subject of intense debate, attracting the intervention of civil society organisations, which in the 1990s exerted immense pressure on the trade and industry in the consuming countries. The civil society campaigns led to the development of various programmes to address the plight of coffee farmers. These initiatives were explicitly concerned with paying a fair price to coffee producers. Although the Fair-trade movement was born in the first part of the 20th century, coffee attracted particular attention during the 1990s. This was the period after the collapse of quotas under the International Coffee Agreement in July 1989, when prices fell to such a low level that it made farmers vulnerable to extreme poverty. There is a call for action to ensure the sustainability of the global industry by enabling the producers to break out of the vicious circle of poverty and attain prosperity.

Fairtrade Minimum Prices

A report came out in March 2023 of the decision by Fairtrade to raise its minimum price for coffee to strengthen protections for farmers around the world. This was in recognition of the severe impacts of climate change on production, leading to increased costs to producers in mitigating the effects of climate change. Fairtrade also recognised that global economic volatility adversely affected farming communities already significantly impacted by wild market fluctuations. Additionally, high inflation in the producer countries significantly increased farmers' costs, especially the costs of adaptation to climate change.

The new Fairtrade prices became effective for contracts signed as of 1st August 2023. These increases would raise the baseline price by 19 per cent and 29 per cent for Fairtrade-certified Robusta and Arabica coffee, respectively. Fairtrade's action was intended to provide farmers with significant price risk management support because of the challenges already highlighted. Fairtrade acknowledges that smallholder farmers are responsible for a significant proportion of global production (60%) — yet half of them live in poverty, and 25% live in extreme poverty. The issue of poverty among coffee farmers is a big problem that even Fairtrade acknowledges cannot be resolved by one organisation alone.

Conclusion

The 2022 Multidimensional Poverty Index (MPI) report notes that reducing poverty through specific actions is possible. The report showed that some new 'poverty profiles' could offer a breakthrough in development efforts in tackling the interlinked aspects. We are made aware of specific recurring patterns of poverty that must be addressed to attain the United Nations Sustainable Development Goals. The series of deprivation bundles identified in the MPI report as patterns in the poverty profiles require specific actions. Where coffee producers are victims, such as in the case of Ethiopia and Uganda, all parties concerned have to act. The available data referenced by the MPI indicates that 1.2 billion people, mostly from developing countries, live in conditions characteristic of acute multidimensional poverty.

As one drinks a cup of coffee, one should ask themselves, "Is there poverty in my cup?" To answer the question, one must know who grew the coffee, the conditions under which they live and if the value chain shows responsibility in caring for the welfare of the producers. It is critical to know if there is multidimensional poverty in the respective coffee-producing communities, to demand transparency and information on the condition of the producers, and what is being done to address the poverty question. The next chapter discusses production, looking at the producing countries and the impact of coffee on the respective economies.

5

The People that Grow the Coffee

Early in 2023, there was a report — actually a set of reports — from one of the global coffee companies summarising the past year's operations and pointing out their accomplishments. It was intriguing to see if there was any mention of the people who grow the coffee. Well, there was in one of the reports, but in a way that ticks the right boxes regarding social and environmental issues where they must show compliance. While keeping the company's name anonymous, it was clear from the reports that much more attention is on meeting investor expectations regarding share value and returns on investment. The managers have to create more value for the investors. They would not keep their jobs if they focused on pleasing the farmers who grow the raw products, because the company operates in a very competitive environment.

This observation is a reality, and most of the time, when producers and consumers are in discussions, there is always a sense of inequity. Sometimes, when the consuer offers assistance, it must be seen as generous and compassionate — but the question is, "Who is it that cannot survive without the other?" Unless some social-entrepreneurial approaches revolutionise the different situations, there is no real sustainability and, thus, no long-term transformational impact.

Recognising the Producer's Plight

Market reality is critical in discussing the plight of the people who grow coffee. Having considered market reality, it is clear that there is a great need to find ways of blessing the people who produce the coffee that we all enjoy. The supply chain has many players, rendering services at different levels. For obvious logistical reasons, the final buyer who goes on to manufacture the finished product does not directly interact with the producers — which is valid for large companies. Nevertheless, they can give back to producers via projects that satisfy corporate social responsibility targets or compliance with legislation in the company's domicile. The exception is that of small operators, such as specialty or gourmet roasters, who can directly engage with the producers or their cooperatives and, most times, even cut out many unnecessary intermediaries. Also, several small or medium-sized coffee-buying companies that supply the roasters in the consuming countries endeavour to establish connections with the producers to build relationships and loyalty in the origins. Some of these companies initiate projects that address specific concerns among the producers, especially the SDG-related objectives and certification programmes.

The Coffee Producers: Who are they?

According to the International Coffee Organization (ICO), coffee is grown commercially in more than 50 countries in the world's tropical regions. Brazil is the leading producer and exporter, accounting for about 40% of global exports. Vietnam is the world's second-largest producer, accounting for about 25% of global exports. The other big producers are Colombia, Indonesia, Ethiopia, Honduras, Uganda, Peru, India, Guatemala, Mexico, Nicaragua, Ivory Coast, and Laos. While some countries produce huge volumes, some produce exceptional quality in smaller volumes, including Kenya, Tanzania, Rwanda, Jamaica, Papua New Guinea, and others. Notably, most coffee is grown by smallholder farmers, some on tiny plots. In most cases, coffee is the most significant contributor to family incomes and livelihoods.

After consuming some of what they produce, the coffee-producing countries export around 130 million bags (60 kg each) in raw form, which is processed and consumed (some processed coffee is re-exported) by the importing countries. In the 2021/22 coffee year, Brazil's green bean exports accounted for almost 30% of the global volumes, while Vietnam had about 22% of global exports—the two countries accounted for more than 50% of total exports. Regarding producer regions, South America (which includes Brazil), with a share of about 43% of global exports, is the largest exporter, while Asia & Oceania is the second biggest with a 34% share. Central America & Mexico have just over 12% of the total exports, and Africa's share is just under 11% of the market. As already noted, the location of the producing countries is within the world's tropical regions — with Africa at the centre, and being the origin of both the Arabica and Robusta varieties.

Africa — the Origin of Coffee

While Africa is the origin of coffee, its share of global production is less than 11%. Ethiopia is widely regarded as the birthplace of coffee, and the Kaffa region, which is located in the southwestern part of the country, is often specifically cited as the origin of coffee. According to Ethiopian legend, a goat herder named Kaldi discovered coffee after noticing his goats becoming energetic from eating the red berries from a certain tree, which turned out to be the coffee plant, which we now know as Arabica coffee. The word "coffee" itself is believed to have derived from the name Kaffa, the region where this discovery took place. This is estimated to have happened around the ninth century AD and the discovery of Arabica coffee changed the world because from Ethiopia, coffee cultivation and consumption spread to various parts of the world, eventually becoming one of the most popular beverages globally. As for Robusta coffee, its origin is in Uganda, where species of wild Robusta still exist and are protected under a biodiversity conservation programme. However, Ethiopia and Uganda are not even among the top four producers, but as we will see later, they are the two African countries that feature among the top 10 world producers. Coffee is nonetheless one of Africa's most important economic crops, though the sector faces challenges. With challenges grouped into four broad categories, Africa has to overcome the following:

- Inefficient production;
- Unpredictable international markets;
- Limited intra-regional trade and investment;
- Infra-structural inefficiencies.

Africa also generally has poor statistics on the agricultural sector, and coffee too suffers the same, though several efforts are being made to address the shortcomings. Historically, in many communities in Eastern and Central Africa, the coffee bean was used for ceremonial purposes. This was typical in the Buganda kingdom (Uganda), the origin of Robusta coffee, where the coffee berries were cooked, dried and chewed as a stimulant, and the entertainment of guests always included coffee to eat. (Yes! This will be explained in Chapter Six). Coffee was also particularly significant in cementing blood covenants between warring parties.

Production inefficiencies are largely responsible for Africa's decline as a producer and export origin, and this matter is being brought to high-level policy discussions to establish how to address the key constraints. There is little to do about the unpredictable international market but something can be done to improve domestic markets and promote local consumption. Much of the coffee consumed in Africa is imported, while most of Africa's exports are in raw form. There is scope for value addition in Africa, given the immense potential for domestic consumption and the large market that can be tapped. Through the resource mobilisation of the African Development Bank (AfDB), the African Export Import Bank (Afreximbank), and other development institutions, with progressive though slow improvement in infrastructure, it is anticipated that revenues from oil and mineral exports will finance the improvement of Africa's infrastructure. Nigeria has shown that it is possible — with local entrepreneur Aliko Dangote's significant investments.

Coffee Production in Brazil

Coffee was introduced in the 18th century and became an important crop in Brazil and a vital export commodity by the middle of the nineteenth century. The country has fourteen major coffee-growing regions, the largest of which is Minas Gerais, accounting for almost half of Brazil's crop. The other significant producing regions include Espírito Santo, São Paulo, Bahia, Rondônia, and Paraná. The typical Brazilian farmer is considerably bigger than their counterparts in other producing countries. A small Brazilian farmer will have, say 10-15 hectares — yet in Africa, such would be considered a prominent or large farmer! As such, Brazilian farmers enjoy economies of scale that most others do not have. The Brazilian industry has also harnessed technology much more than any other producing country, with a significantly higher level of mechanisation and much lower production costs than in Africa. However, there are also reports of poverty among some Brazilian farmers, particularly in Bahia state, in the locality of Planalto de Vitória da Conquista.

Brazil is the world's second-largest consumer, as a country, after the United States. Brazilians were not known for coffee consumption until the 1990s when local coffee companies launched an aggressive campaign to promote domestic consumption, which has paid off well. Industry estimates put the per capita consumption at 4.84 kg per year of roasted coffee. Domestic demand has continued to grow, and reports indicate that consumption increased by more than one million bags over the ten years to 2023.

As the Brazilian economy grows and disposable incomes improve, there is speculation that Brazil could overtake the United States as the world's leading consumer (in terms of volume, not per capita consumption). Moreover, Brazil provides some ground-breaking innovations focusing on furthering developments in the soluble coffee industry. The Brazilian Association of Soluble Coffee Industry, which in Portuguese is **Associação Brasileira da Indústria de Café Solúvel** (ABICS), an organisation that represents the soluble coffee industry has made significant achievements over the years. ABICS focuses on improvements in quality, sustainability, technological innovation, and expanding markets for Brazilian soluble coffee. The ABICS white paper that explains the innovation in the grading and classification of instant coffee is discussed in Chapter Eight.

The ABICS was created in 1972 and represents seven Brazilian instant coffee manufacturers that, together, have the largest instant manufacturing capacity in the world. ABICS members include

Cacique, Companhia Iguacu de Café Soluvel, Nestlé, Cocam, Realcafé and Café Campinho, and Olam Food Ingredients. Brazil has been a leader in producing and exporting soluble coffee since the 1960s. According to 2020 figures from Cecafé – the Council of Coffee Exporters of Brazil – and ABICS, Brazil's production of soluble coffee is 117,000 tonnes annually. It exports 4.1 million bags of instant coffee per year, estimated to be worth US$600 million, and distributes 0.95 million bags to Brazil's domestic market.

Coffee Production in Vietnam

Vietnam is the world's second-largest producer, after Brazil. It produces mainly Robusta coffee, which accounts for between 95% and 97% of its total output year-on-year. However, there is an increase Arabica, mostly growing in the north-west part of the country, such as Son La and Dien Bien provinces. Total coffee area is 710,000 hectares. According to the USDA, Vietnam produced 31.58 million bags (green bean equivalent) in the marketing year 2021/2022 and exported 27 million bags, which is about 85% of the production. Vietnam has been one of the world's largest producers and exporters for over two decades. Production has steadily increased over the years, with Vietnam's favourable climate and suitable regions for cultivation contributing to its success. Robusta is a favourite in Vietnam due to its higher productivity, resilience to pests and diseases, and suitability for the Vietnamese growing conditions. Vietnam's main coffee production regions are the Central Highlands, North Vietnam, and South Vietnam. The coffee sector in Vietnam employs about 550,000 smallholder farmers, engaging about one million people.

Regarding regional concentration, cultivation is concentrated in the central highlands region, particularly in the provinces of Dak Lak, Lam Dong, Gia Lai, Dak Nong, and Kon Tum. These areas have the ideal climate, altitude, and soil conditions for coffee cultivation. Other coffee-growing regions include the northern mountainous provinces and the southern provinces of Dong Nai and Binh Phuoc. Smallholder farmers, who own relatively small plots of land, account for most of Vietnam's production. They often employ family labour and adopt traditional cultivation practices. However, there has been an increasing shift towards more modern and sustainable farming techniques, including the use of improved varieties, proper processing methods, and environmental conservation practices. The interventions of global companies such as Nestlé, JDE, Olam, Dak man, Tchibo, Neumann Kaffe Gruppe, Volcafe and others have contributed to transforming production and processing systems and helped professionalise the Vietnamese coffee industry and significantly improve its quality.

A significant proportion of Vietnam's crop is "dry processed" which involves drying the coffee cherries as soon as they are harvested and then milling to remove the husks. The rest of the coffee is "wet processed", also known as the washing method, where the cherries are pulped, fermented, and washed to remove the mucilage before drying — imparting a distinct flavour profile to Vietnamese coffee. Both methods of processing are common across coffee-producing countries. After processing (grading the coffee beans according to their size), the green coffee is packed in 60-kg bags or bulk containers and then exported. Countries like the United States, Germany, Italy, Spain, and Japan are major importers of Vietnamese coffee.

In recent years, again, thanks to the efforts of international coffee companies and non-governmental organisations, there has been a growing emphasis on sustainability in Vietnam's coffee industry. Various initiatives focus on promoting sustainable cultivation practices, improving farmer livelihoods, and addressing environmental challenges like deforestation and water pollution. As a major producer, its production systems must comply with international environmental sustainability requirements. Thus, the government, coffee associations, and international organisations have worked together to support sustainable coffee production in Vietnam, and this effort was still going on by the end of 2023.

The Vietnamese industry has not been without challenges, which include fluctuating international coffee prices, climate change impacts on coffee cultivation, pest and disease management, the need for quality enhancement and improved infrastructure and processing facilities. The COVID-19 pandemic also affected production and trade, leading to some disruptions in the supply chain and market demand. Despite these challenges, Vietnam's industry plays a significant role in the country's economy and the global coffee market. The combination of favourable growing conditions, a robust supply chain, and increasing sustainability efforts positions Vietnam as a significant player in the global industry.

Coffee Production in Colombia

Colombia, the third largest producer after Brazil and Vietnam, is known for its high-quality Arabica coffee beans. Colombia exclusively cultivates Arabica, known for its excellent flavour and aroma. The country's diverse microclimates, volcanic soils, and ideal altitude contribute to the production of premium Arabica beans. Cultivation is spread across various regions, each offering unique characteristics that influence the flavour profile of the beans. Some notable regions include Antioquia, Tolima, Huila, Cauca, Nariño, Quindio, and Caldas, with each having its own distinct terroir and producing coffee with different flavour profiles.

Production primarily involves smallholder farmers, often owning less than five hectares of land. They are typically members of cooperatives or associations which support them with resources, technical assistance, and market access. Smallholder farms contribute to the overall diversity and high-quality nature of Colombian coffee. The country has established strict quality control measures and grading systems to ensure consistency and excellence. Colombian coffee has a high standing in the specialty coffee market, and the country has gained a reputation for producing unique and distinct flavour profiles. The coffee cultural landscape in Colombia's *Coffee Triangle* region (comprising Caldas, Quindio, and Risaralda) is a UNESCO World Heritage site. The region is recognised for its exceptional coffee landscapes, traditional farming practices, and of cultural significance to coffee production.

Colombian producers have been hailed for adopting sustainable farming practices, which include promoting agroforestry systems, organic farming methods, and environmentally friendly production techniques. Certifications such as Fairtrade, Rainforest Alliance, and Organic are common. However, production faces challenges such as fluctuations in international coffee prices, climate change impacts (including unpredictable weather patterns and diseases like coffee rust), limited access to financing for farm renovation, and the need for technological advancements to improve efficiency and productivity. Through the National Federation of Coffee Growers of Colombia (FNC), the Colombian government provides a wide range of support to farmers. Such support includes technical assistance, research and development, marketing efforts, and initiatives to improve farmer livelihoods. The industry plays a significant role in the country's economy, cultural heritage, and international coffee market. The commitment to producing high-quality Arabica beans, using sustainable practices, and preserving the Coffee Cultural Landscape have all helped maintain Colombia's reputation as a top producer nation.

Coffee Production in Indonesia

After Brazil, Vietnam, and Colombia, Indonesia is the world's fourth-largest producer and exporter, and the sector has 1.77 million smallholder farmers in production. The principal coffee production regions are Sumatra, Java, Sulawesi and Bali. In 2020, Indonesia produced 10.9 million 60-kilogram bags, which increased to about 12.9 million bags in 2021.

The country is one of the most diverse coffee origins in the world, producing both Arabica and Robusta coffee. Robusta accounts for about 85% of total output. However, most of Indonesia's Arabicas have been categorised as specialty coffee and receive premium prices. Several types, such as Sumatra, are also labelled with geographic indications, gaining the advantage of differentiation in the market. More than 32 areas are registered at the Ministry of Law and Human Rights of the Republic of Indonesia as Geographical Indications products.

Indonesia contributes 5% of the world's coffee exports, its main export destinations being the United States, Germany, Japan and Malaysia. However, other exports like oil palm and rubber contribute significantly more to the national economy, and cereal crops are the primary focus of most public research and development investment. In the decade to 2023, coffee's share of agricultural GDP has fallen by nearly two-thirds.

Nonetheless, Indonesia has a growing domestic coffee market, with domestic consumption estimated at 10 per cent of its annual production, where the domestic coffee value chain development has become significant in employment creation. Indonesia has a higher domestic consumption of coffee than most producing countries.

Coffee Production in Ethiopia

Ethiopia is reputed to be Africa's biggest coffee producer, as well as the leading consumer. Accurate statistics are unavailable, but estimates indicate that Ethiopians consume more than half of their production. Ethiopia is the origin of Arabica coffee and remains one of the world's major high-quality producers. The heirloom varieties of Arabica stand out. The highly prized Arabica beans boast exceptional quality, diverse flavour profiles, and distinct regional characteristics. The country is a significant exporter of coffee, which is a crucial source of foreign exchange earnings. Ethiopian coffee is sought after globally and is often labelled with its regional names, highlighting the specific origin and flavour characteristics.

Cultivation happens across several regions, each known for producing unique coffee profiles. Some notable regions include Sidamo, Yirgacheffe, Guji, Harrar, Limu, Jimma, and Gedeo. These have varying altitudes, microclimates, and soil compositions, contributing to the diversity of the country's produce. Production is primarily carried out by smallholder farmers, often working on family-owned plots of land. They employ traditional practices, including shade-grown coffee under diverse agroforestry systems. Ethiopia has a high number of coffee-growing households, an important source of income for many rural communities. Ethiopia is famous for its unique coffee processing method called "natural" or "dry", where coffee cherries are dried whole, allowing the beans to ferment inside the fruit. This imparts distinct fruity and wine-like flavours to Ethiopian coffees. However, a good proportion of Ethiopian coffee is wet-processed.

Many Ethiopian farmers are organised into cooperatives, and cooperatives into unions that support and represent their interests. Coffee cooperative unions play a significant role in the industry and help with collective marketing, fair trade practices, and access to resources, including training, financing, and infrastructure development. These cooperative unions work to support and empower smallholder coffee farmers, promote sustainable farming practices, improve quality standards, and facilitate the marketing and export of Ethiopian coffee. Some of the prominent cooperative unions are:

Oromia Coffee Farmers' Cooperative Union (OCFCU) — one of Ethiopia's largest, it represents over 400,000 farmers across the Oromia region. The OCFCU is also known for producing high-quality coffee. It focuses on improving farmers' livelihoods through fair trade practices and ensuring sustainable production;

Sidama Coffee Farmers' Cooperative Union (SCFCU) — based in the Sidama region, which is renowned for coffee-growing areas such as Sidamo. It represents thousands of coffee farmers and promotes sustainable practices, quality control, and direct market access for its members;

Yirgacheffe Coffee Farmers' Cooperative Union (YCFCU) — it is dedicated to promoting and supporting the farmers of the Yirgacheffe area. This area produces some of Ethiopia's finest coffee. It aims to maintain the unique qualities and traceability of Yirgacheffe coffee while ensuring fair compensation for farmers;

Kaffa Forest Coffee Farmers' Cooperative Union (KFCFCU) — it operates in the Southwestern region. KFCFCU works to preserve coffee forests' biodiversity and natural habitat while promoting sustainable coffee farming practices. The cooperative union assists farmers in accessing markets and obtaining fair prices; and

Bale Mountain Coffee Farmers' Cooperative Union (BMCF-CU) — operates in the Bale Mountains in Oromia region. These mountains are a UNESCO Biosphere Reserve known for its rich biodiversity. The cooperative union works with farmers to enhance production, quality, and sustainability while preserving the natural environment.

The above are just a few examples of the country's cooperative unions. Each union serves as a vital support system for coffee farmers, enabling them to access markets, improve their livelihoods, and contribute to preserving Ethiopia's rich heritage. Because production faces various challenges, the unions' support is critical. Challenges include limited access to financing, inadequate infrastructure, climate change impacts (such as droughts and shifting rainfall patterns), pests and diseases (including coffee berry disease and coffee leaf rust), and market price fluctuations. Support from the government and various development partners, who work closely with the cooperatives, helps to address the various challenges. Through the Ethiopian Coffee and Tea Authority (ECTA) and other institutions, the government promotes the sector's development and growth with efforts like quality improvement programmes, certification initiatives (such as Organic and Fairtrade), and supporting cooperatives and smallholder farmers.

Coffee holds deep cultural significance in Ethiopia, ingrained in the country's history, traditions, and social fabric. The coffee ceremony, a ritualised process of brewing and serving coffee, is a symbol of hospitality, friendship, and community bonding. Ethiopia's rich heritage, diverse varieties, and traditional production methods contribute to its reputation as a unique and important player in the global industry. The country continues to focus on sustainable practices, market access, and value addition to further strengthen its coffee sector and benefit its grower communities.

Coffee Production in Honduras

According to the US Department of Agriculture (USDA), Honduras is the largest coffee producer in Central America, the third largest in Latin America, and has experienced significant growth in its coffee industry over the years. Honduras ranks fifth in global production. Honduran production in marketing year (MY) 2021/22 (Oct 2021 to Sept 2022) was forecast at 5.5 million 60-kilogram bags, a 12% decrease from the previous year due to weather conditions and leaf rust disease. Honduras produces mainly Arabica coffee, with 61% of farms located between 3,900 and 5,200 feet (1,189-1,585 metres) above sea level. The crop is one of the most important sources of livelihood for rural populations and significantly contributes to the nation's economy, providing employment opportunities and generating export revenue. The country exports a substantial portion of its production to international markets, including the United States, Germany, Belgium, and Japan.

Honduras's coffee is known for its high quality and desirable flavour profiles. The country grows diverse Arabica varieties, including Typica, Bourbon, Caturra, and Catuai. Coffee is grown in various regions, with the main producing areas located in the western and central parts of the country. Notable regions include Copan, Santa Barbara, Ocotepeque, Comayagua, and El Paraiso. Each one has distinct microclimates and altitudes, contributing to the unique characteristics of the coffee. Production is predominantly by smallholder farmers who own relatively small plots of land. The farmers often belong to cooperatives or associations that provide them with technical support, access to financing, and market opportunities. Smallholder farming contributes to the social and economic development of rural communities.

Honduras has gained recognition for its organic and specialty coffee production. Many farms have adopted organic farming practices, emphasising environmental sustainability and the production of high-quality, niche crops. Specialty coffee from Honduras has been awarded international accolades for its unique flavours and cup profiles. Processing includes both washed (wet) and natural (dry) processing methods. Washed processing involves removing the outer fruit layer before drying the beans, resulting in cleaner and brighter flavour profiles. Natural processing involves drying the coffee cherries whole, allowing the beans to develop unique fruity and wine-like flavours.

Honduras faces several challenges in coffee production, including the impact of climate change, such as irregular rainfall patterns, increased incidence of pests and diseases (e.g., coffee leaf rust), and vulnerability to natural disasters. Additionally, limited access to financing, outdated infrastructure, and market price fluctuations pose challenges to the sector's growth and stability. Through organisations like the Honduran Coffee Institute (IHCAFE), the government provides support and resources to farmers. Efforts include technical assistance, training programmes, access to credit, and initiatives to improve productivity, quality, and market access. Honduras continues to invest in the development of its sector, focusing on improving quality, sustainability, and market competitiveness. Efforts are underway to mitigate the challenges faced by farmers, enhance productivity, and ensure the long-term viability of production.

Coffee Production in Uganda

Uganda is a leading coffee-producing country in East Africa with a long coffee culture history. Coffee is Uganda's top-earning export crop. In 2011, the country became Africa's top producer of Robusta coffee. Uganda produces both Arabica and Robusta coffee, with 80% of the production being Robusta. Arabica is grown in the highland areas on the slopes of Mount Elgon in the East and Mt. Rwenzori and Mt. Muhabura in the South Western Region. Robusta grows natively in the central plateau areas of the Lake Victoria basin and in Kibale Forest in Western Uganda. In this protected area, different species of wild coffee, including Robusta, still grow. The Uganda Coffee Development Authority (UCDA) was formed in 1991 by an Act of Parliament, when the industry was liberalised, removing the monopoly of the government-controlled Coffee Marketing Board and opening up space to private exporters. Reports from UCDA show positive trends in production, improvements in yields and quality enhancement at all levels.

Robusta coffee thrives in Uganda's climate and soil conditions. Robusta is hailed for its higher yields, disease resistance, and suitability for lower altitudes. Coffee is grown in various regions of Uganda, with the major coffee-producing areas including the western, central, and eastern regions. Notable growing regions include the central and southwestern regions, Mt. Elgon, Rwenzori, and West Nile. Although Robusta dominates, Uganda also cultivates Arabica coffee, primarily in the Mount Elgon region in the eastern part of the country and other high-altitude areas in the highlands of the western part of the country. Each region has distinct microclimates and soil characteristics that influence the flavours and profiles of the produce.

While Arabica production is done to a lesser extent, it is gaining attention for its potential in specialty coffee markets. Uganda's production is primarily carried out by smallholder farmers, often working on small plots of land. These farmers form cooperatives or associations that provide them with technical support, access to markets, and training on sustainable farming practices. Smallholder farming contributes to rural livelihoods and plays a significant role in the country's coffee sector. Uganda's coffee processing includes wet (washed) and dry (natural) processing methods.

The industry faces various challenges, including inadequate infrastructure; limited access to financing and market information; fluctuating international coffee prices; pests and diseases (such as coffee wilt disease and coffee berry disease); and climate change impacts like irregular rainfall patterns and rising temperatures. Addressing these challenges is crucial for the sector's growth and resilience. The government provides support to coffee farmers through agencies like the UCDA, including technical assistance, capacity-building programmes, research and development initiatives, and market promotion efforts. Café Africa Uganda has been working in partnership with UCDA since 2006, first in establishing the Uganda Coffee Platform. The Platform is an industry coalition that brings together different players to discuss sector-related issues. Café Africa also supports capacity building by promoting good agricultural and agronomic practices, developing extension training materials, and specifically building the capacity of the youth in coffee. The government aims to enhance productivity, improve quality, and expand market opportunities for Ugandan coffee.

The crop is vital to Uganda's economy, providing employment opportunities, foreign exchange earnings, and rural development.

Uganda exports a significant portion of its coffee, with major export destinations including the European Union, Sudan, South Sudan, and the United States. The industry continues to evolve, with efforts to improve productivity, enhance quality, and promote sustainability. The government is focusing on improving the efficiency of smallholder farming and diversification of coffee varieties — to introduce more disease-resistant, high-yielding and drought-tolerant varieties. The government also explicitly focuses on promoting value addition that will spur opportunities for the sector's growth and improve farmers' livelihoods.

Coffee Production in India

Coffee production in India is significant, as the country is one of the major global producers. India is known for its specialty coffee varieties, including Arabica and Robusta, and the coffee industry plays an important role in the agricultural sector. The production of coffee lies primarily in the southern states — in the hills of the southern region — of which Karnataka accounts for the highest yield. The states of Kerala and Tamil Nadu are the other major producers. Within the above states are specific districts and regions known for their coffee cultivation, such as Chikmagalur, Coorg, Wayanad, Nilgiris, and Araku Valley.

India grows Arabica in higher altitudes, typically above 2,000 feet, and Robusta at lower altitudes. Each variety has its own characteristics and flavour profiles, contributing to the diversity of Indian produce. Indian coffee is grown in the shade and has a reputation as one of the finest shade-grown coffee in the world. India has about 379,697 coffee growers, with 98% of them being small scale farmers. The estimated production for the season 2021/2022 was over 352,000 metric tons, with almost 60 per cent of Indian coffee being exported. Germany, USA, Russia, Spain, and Italy are its largest markets.

One of the most famous Indian varieties is Monsooned Malabar. It is a uniquely processed coffee where the green beans are exposed to the monsoon winds and moisture, resulting in a distinct flavour profile characterised by low acidity, earthy notes, and a mellow taste. Production involves a combination of smallholder farmers and large plantations. Smallholder farmers often grow coffee alongside other crops, while plantations are dedicated coffee farms with organised cultivation and processing systems.

Many Indian farms follow sustainable and environmentally friendly practices. Shade-grown coffee is is produced by cultivating plants under the shade of taller trees, preserving biodiversity and creating a favourable habitat for birds and other wildlife. Additionally, there is a growing trend of organic coffee production, with farms adopting organic farming methods and obtaining organic certifications. Processing methods vary depending on the region and coffee variety. Common processing techniques include washed (wet) processing, natural (dry) processing, and the unique 'monsooning' process for Malabar coffee, outlined above.

A significant proportion of India's coffee is consumed domestically. Coffee is a popular beverage, and its consumption has increased over the years. Production has a rich history and continues to thrive, with a focus on quality, sustainability, and specialty coffee. The country's diverse growing regions, unique processing methods, and dedication to preserving traditional practices contribute to the overall reputation and success of Indian coffee in the global market.

Coffee Production in Peru

According to the ICO, Peru is one of the world's top 10 coffee producers. It ranks fifth in the export of Arabica. Peru predominantly produces Arabica and only a limited amount of Robusta coffee. Over 70% Peru's Arabica is of the '*typica*' variety followed by '*caturra*' (20%), and others (10%). Arabica is grown in the highland areas on the slopes of the Andes, while Robusta grows in the lowland areas near the Amazon River. Coffee production played a role in the country's history and is important for the national economy. According to USDA reports, Peruvian coffee production in marketing year (MY) 2022/2023 (Oct 2022 to Sept 2023) was 4.03 million 60-kilogram bags, an increase of two per cent from the previous year due to favourable weather conditions and improved agronomic practices. Peru's exports in MY 2022/23 were forecast at 3.95 million 60-kilogram bags, a slight increase from the previous year. The United States continued to be the top market.

Coffee Production in Guatemala

Guatemala began coffee production in the 1850s, and the country became Central America's top producer for most of the 20th century and the beginning of the 21st, when it was overtaken by Honduras in 2011. Nonetheless, coffee is still a significant cash crop Guatemala's economy. It has a long history of cultivation and is renowned for its high-quality Arabica beans. Guatemala's diverse geography and microclimates contribute to the cultivation of exceptional coffee. The most prominent growing regions include Antigua, Atitlán, Huehuetenango, Cobán, and Fraijanes. Each region has its own unique characteristics and flavour profiles. Guatemala predominantly cultivates Arabica coffee, which is prized for its nuanced flavours, acidity, and aroma.

The country grows various Arabica varieties, including Bourbon, Typica, Caturra, Catuai, and Pacamara, each offering distinct flavours and characteristics. The volcanic soil is rich in minerals and provides excellent growing conditions. Volcanic regions, such as Antigua, are known for their fertile soil, which contributes to the unique flavour profiles of the coffee beans. Production involves a mix of large estates, cooperative farms, and smallholder farmers. Many coffee farms are family-owned and operated, with a focus on traditional farming practices and preserving the quality of their crop. Guatemala has a strong tradition of shade-grown coffee, in which plants are cultivated under the shade of larger trees, providing a natural canopy that protects the coffee plants from direct sunlight and encourages biodiversity on the farms.

Most Guatemalan coffee is processed using the wet processing method, known for producing clean and vibrant flavours. Guatemala has gained a reputation for producing specialty coffee. Their beans score high on the Specialty Coffee Association (SCA) scoring system, indicating their exceptional quality and unique attributes. Guatemala has several coffee cooperative organisations that support smallholder farmers and promote sustainable farming practices. They help farmers access resources, improve coffee quality, and facilitate direct trade relationships with international buyers. Guatemala's coffee industry is highly regarded globally, with its beans prized for their balanced acidity, full body, and distinct flavour profiles. The country's commitment to quality, traditional farming methods, and focus on sustainable practices has contributed to its position as a top coffee origin and a preferred choice for specialty coffee enthusiasts.

Coffee Production in Mexico

Mexico is a coffee-producing country in North America. In 2019/20, Mexico produced around 3.7 million 60-kilogram bags, a year-on-year increase of 4.2%. Mexico is known for its rich coffee heritage and diverse growing regions. Mexico produces

Arabica, which grows particularly well in the coastal region of Soconusco, Chiapas, near the border of Guatemala but also produces small quantities of Robusta. There are 15 coffee-producing states in Mexico: Chiapas, which leads with 40% of production, Veracruz at 25%, and Puebla at 16%, while the rest is produced mainly in Oaxaca, Nayarit, and Guerrero. The different growing regions offer diverse microclimates, altitudes, and soil types that contribute to the variety of Mexican coffee.

Mexico's coffee farms are situated at varying altitudes, ranging from around 800 to 1,800 metres above sea level. The altitude plays a crucial role in flavour development, with higher altitudes generally associated with more complex and flavorful coffee profiles. Many coffee farms in Mexico embrace sustainable and organic farming practices. Mexico is a significant producer of certified organic coffee, and farmers focus on preserving the environment, maintaining biodiversity, and protecting natural resources. Mexico has a strong presence of coffee cooperatives, which play a vital role in supporting smallholder farmers. These cooperatives help farmers access resources, provide technical assistance, and facilitate fair trade practices, ensuring better livelihoods for the farmers.

Mexican coffee includes a range of Arabica varieties, including Typica, Bourbon, Caturra, and Mundo Novo. Some regions have specific varietal distinctions, such as Pluma and Altura coffee from the Chiapas region. Additionally, Mexico produces various coffee blends tailored to different taste preferences and market demands. Traditional processing methods are, washed (wet) processing and natural (dry) processing. These methods contribute to the flavour profiles and characteristics of Mexican coffee. The country has a significant domestic coffee consumption culture, with the beverage being integral to daily life. Additionally, Mexico exports a substantial amount, with the United States being one of the primary export markets. Mexico's industry showcases a rich diversity of flavours, growing regions, and cultural significance. From the high-altitude coffee farms of Chiapas to the vibrant communities in Oaxaca, Mexican coffee offers a range of taste experiences and reflects the country's proud coffee heritage.

Coffee Production in Nicaragua

Nicaragua was listed by the World Atlas in 2019 as the world's 12th largest exporter, with 2.9 million 60kg bags. Coffee production in the 2020/2021 marketing year experienced a 15 per cent drop compared to the previous year. It was noted that coffee plantations were poorly maintained due to the limited access to credit and the impact of hurricanes ETA and IOTA during the 2020/2021 coffee harvest, all contributing to the decline in production. The Nicaraguan coffee sector employs more than 5% of the population, 330,000 people, with an average Nicaraguan farm being roughly five hectares. The country has had a history of social and political unrest that significantly impacted its economy and the development of its coffee industry.

Coffee is mainly produced in the North Central Region, with a range of altitudes from 365 to 1,500 metres above sea level. The areas most suitable for the cultivation of coffee have been Managua Department, Diriamba, San Marcos, and Jinotepe, as well as the vicinity of Granada Department, Lake Nicaragua, Chontales Department, and in Nueva Segovia. Historically, the best coffee is produced in Matagalpa and in Jinotega. Nicaraguan coffees are characterised as bright, citric acidity, a smooth body, and floral, citrus, or chocolate flavours, giving them unique national profiling. However, specific flavour profiles vary from one region to another depending on the different microclimates.

The industry built a reputation, particularly among North American consumers, beginning with the introduction of the Cup of Excellence in 2002, which led to a significant focus on quality and drew the interest of international buyers. As a result, the attention of several international buyers has increasingly been drawn to Nicaragua as a coffee origin. The varieties, which include Marogogipe, Pacamara, Bourbon, Catuai, Geisha, and Pacas, are similar to those found in the other countries in Central America. These varieties thrive in the country's range of microclimates, thus providing prospective buyers with a wide choice for developing their blends. Nicaragua has also made significant investments in the development of Robusta production, whose effect will be seen in due course.

Coffee Production in Ivory Coast (Côte d'Ivoire)

Coffee production is an important aspect of Côte d'Ivoire's economy, and it continues to strengthen its economic backbone, for instance by boosting rural employment and being a vital export commodity. While coffee has its origins in Africa, with the discovery of Arabica coffee in the Kaffa region of Ethiopia during ancient times, and Robusta coffee in the eastern and central African equatorial forests, coffee trees did not arrive on the other side of the continent at the Ivory Coast until the 19th century. When Côte d'Ivoire was a French territory, the French brought in coffee tree seedlings, and commercial production commenced. Following World War II, coffee production increased from 36,000 tons in 1945 to 112,500 tons in 1958. Production subsequently expanded, and Côte d'Ivoire became the largest producer in Africa in the 1970s and 1980s, and one of the largest sources of Robusta in the world. Unfortunately, the social and political upheavals of the 1990s and the first decade of the 21st century had long-lasting negative effects on the Ivorian coffee industry. Vietnam, Indonesia, and Uganda superseded Ivorian production, and the West African country lost its position among the world's top 10 producers.

Coffee Production in Laos

Laos produces approximately 30,000 tonnes annually, about one-third of them being Arabica beans and the rest Robusta. Production has been growing steadily over the years, and the country is emerging as a notable coffee origin in Southeast Asia. The crop is predominantly grown in the southern part of Laos, particularly in the Bolaven Plateau region. The Bolaven Plateau is known for its favourable altitude, climate, and volcanic soil, creating ideal conditions. Arabica is typically grown at higher altitudes, while Robusta is cultivated at lower elevations. The Bolaven Plateau is known for its high-quality Arabica coffee, with flavours ranging from fruity and floral to chocolatey and nutty.

Coffee production is largely carried out by smallholder farmers who often employ traditional and organic farming practices, contributing to Laotian coffee's unique character and sustainability. Coffee cooperatives and associations provide resources, training, and market access to small-scale producers, helping them improve quality and connect with international buyers. Traditional coffee farming practices include shade-grown cultivation, with plants growing under the shade of larger trees, providing natural protection against excessive sunlight and promoting biodiversity on the farms. Processing is typically the application of both wet and dry methods. Each method contributes to the flavour characteristics of Laotian coffee.

Laos has seen an increasing focus on organic coffee production, with farmers adopting sustainable farming practices and obtaining organic certifications. The country also produces specialty coffee, with an emphasis on quality, traceability, and unique flavour profiles. While consumption within Laos is growing, the country also exports a significant portion of its produce, to various international markets, including Europe, the United States, and neighbouring Southeast Asian countries. The industry is still developing, and the country's unique geography, dedication to quality, and growing focus on sustainability position it as an emerging player in the specialty market. Laotian coffee offers a distinct flavour profile and provides economic opportunities for smallholder farmers, contributing to the country's agricultural landscape and rural livelihoods.

Other Coffee-Producing Countries

The other producers, not listed among the top exporters yet producing exceptional coffees, include Costa Rica, Tanzania, Kenya, Rwanda, Cameroon, the Democratic Republic of Congo, Malawi, Jamaica, and Papua New Guinea, although the list is not exhaustive.

Costa Rica has a great reputation as a producer of high-quality coffee. The crop contributes significantly to the economy. According to the USDA Foreign Agricultural Service, Costa Rica's marketing year 2020/2021 production reached 1,472,202 60-kilogramme (kg) bags, which was 0.4% higher than the previous crop, and projections for 2021/2022 showed a slight increase to about 1,485,000 bags. Costa Rica's diverse microclimates, volcanic soils, and altitude variations contribute to the production of specialty coffees with distinct flavours and profiles. Cultivating regions are spread throughout the country, with notable areas including Tarrazú, Tres Ríos, Central Valley, and West Valley. Each region has its own characteristics and produces coffee with unique attributes. Costa Rica is committed to sustainable coffee production practices. Many farmers adopt environmentally friendly techniques. The use of shade trees, organic fertilisers, and integrated pest management systems is common. Additionally, some farms have obtained certifications such as Rainforest Alliance and Fair Trade, demonstrating their commitment to social and environmental responsibility.

The Costa Rican coffee industry is known for its focus on quality. Beans are typically hand-picked to ensure only ripe cherries are harvested. After harvesting, the beans undergo careful processing, including methods such as wet processing (washing) or honey processing, which contribute to the coffee's flavour and characteristics. The Coffee Institute of Costa Rica (ICAFE) supports the industry, providing farmers with technical assistance, research, and education, promoting sustainability practices, and overseeing quality control measures. Farmers in Costa Rica grapple with weather, pests, diseases, and market fluctuations. Still, ICAFE has a significant database and information dissemination that helps the farmers under their organisation, the Costa Rican Coffee Growers Association (CoopeTarrazú R.L).

Tanzania is the third largest coffee producer in Eastern Africa, after Ethiopia and Uganda, producing both Arabica and Robusta varieties. The country has a significant agricultural sector, and coffee is vital to its economy. Annual production in Tanzania fluctuates due to weather conditions, farming practices, and market dynamics. Café Africa supports the Tanzanian National Coffee Platform, an initiative that brings together the various players in the sector. Over the last few years, production averaged around one million 60-kilogram bags annually. The coffee is grown in various regions, including Kilimanjaro, Mbeya, Arusha, and Kagera. These regions have favourable altitudes, soil, and climatic factors that contribute to the production of specialty-grade coffee.

The Kilimanjaro area is famous for some of Tanzania's finest coffees, grown around Mount Kilimanjaro, Africa's tallest mountain. Although not many are aware of this fact, Mt Kilimanjaro is the world's tallest free-standing mountain (not part of a mountain range, given that Mt Everest — the world's tallest — is part of a mountain range). It is significant and worth noting that Mt Kilimanjaro has similarities to Mount Fuji in Japan. Mt Kilimanjaro is a giant dormant stratovolcano composed of three distinct volcanic cones: Kibo, the highest at 5,895 metres (19,340 ft); Mawenzi, at 5,149 metres (16,893 ft); and Shira, the lowest at 4,005 metres (13,140 ft). Mount Fuji, located on the island of Honshū, is the highest mountain in Japan, with a summit elevation of 3,776.24 metres (12,389 ft 3 in). A few decades ago, Tanzania coffee became famous in Japan, owing to the story about Mt Kilimanjaro due to its resemblance to Mount Fuji. Thus, Kilimanjaro coffee conjured positive emotions — and still does — among some Japanese consumers nostalgic about the resemblance of the two mountains.

Kenya is a well-known coffee origin with a reputation for some of the finest coffees on the market. It is the fourth producer and exporter in Eastern Africa. The country was also well-known for its cooperative production system, well-controlled processing and milling, and an auction system that delivered high prices as traders competed for high-quality coffee lots. About 70% of Kenyan coffee is produced by smallholders, with estimates of about 150,000 farmers in Kenya as of 2020. Most of Kenya's coffee is grown around the Mount Kenya area, where the volcanic soils contribute to the unique quality of the produce. Mount Kenya, a volcano located immediately south of the Equator, is the highest mountain in Kenya and the second-highest in Africa, after Kilimanjaro. The highest peaks are Batian (5,199 metres or 17,057 feet), Nelion (5,188 m or 17,021 ft) and Point Lenana (4,985 m or 16,355 ft). Mount Kenya was added to UNESCO's World Heritage List in 1997. Unfortunately, Kenya's coffee declined significantly over the years, with current production only around 40,000 tons, down from a peak of 129,000 tonnes three decades ago.

The decline in Kenya's coffee production can be attributed to several factors, including urbanisation, where coffee farms were converted into real estate. The key turning point was when, as part of the liberalisation process, a new coffee law repealed a provision in the previous law that prohibited the cutting down of a coffee tree. More lucrative agribusiness activities, such as horticulture, competed with and replaced coffee holdings, further reducing the area under coffee production. Other factors included climate change, weak coffee sector systems, poor extension services, and fluctuating global prices against rising costs of production — including agro-inputs and labour — and the rising cost of living for farmers generally.

Rwanda's evolution into a noticeable origin of fine coffee over the past two decades is remarkable. Rwanda's annual production ranges from 20,000 to 22,000 metric tons, mostly Arabica, where the Bourbon variety plants comprise 95% of all coffee trees cultivated in Rwanda. The nation has had a painful history that affected almost all aspects of life, culminating in one of the worst genocides in African history. In recent years, Rwanda has emerged as a significant player in the specialty coffee industry. Coffee production has become an essential source of income for many farmers. Rwanda coffee is appreciated for its high quality and distinct flavour profiles. Production is concentrated in several regions, including the districts of Huye, Gakenke, Nyamasheke, and Rulindo, among others. The country's volcanic soils, high altitudes, and favourable climate provide good conditions for growing specialty coffee.

Coffee farming is predominantly carried out by smallholder farmers who own small plots of land. The government and various organisations have implemented initiatives to support these farmers, including training, access to financing, and technical assistance. These initiatives aim to improve coffee quality, increase productivity, and enhance farmers' livelihoods. Processing methods are often meticulous. Most farmers employ a wet processing method, which helps ensure that they produce clean coffee with vibrant flavours.

One notable aspect of the country's industry is the emphasis on sustainability and social impact. Many coffee cooperatives and organisations prioritise fair trade practices, promote gender equality, and invest in community development projects. These initiatives have helped empower farmers, improve living conditions, and foster a more inclusive coffee sector. Rwandan coffee has gained recognition internationally, particularly in the specialty segment. The country has won numerous awards and accolades for its high-quality coffees, including Cup of Excellence competitions. The unique flavour profile, characterised by floral and fruity notes, has contributed to its growing popularity among coffee enthusiasts. Nevertheless, the Rwandan coffee industry still grapples with some challenges, including limited financing access, infrastructure limitations, climate change impacts, and fluctuating international prices. Various organisations and government entities spearheaded by the National Agricultural Export Development Board (NAEB) are working to address these challenges and ensure sustainability and continued growth.

Cameroon's coffee story is a sad one. According to ICO statistics, Cameroon was once Africa's second-largest producer and exporter, with annual production figures as high as 132,000 metric tonnes in the mid-1980s. In fact, the highest yield ever recorded, reported in 1990, was 156,000 metric tonnes. Production fell by almost 50%, from over 65,000 to just over 36,000 tonnes between 2000 and 2010. From 2010 till 2023, production had not recovered but remained low, never passing the 40,000 metric tonne mark, with the worst production of barely 22,000 tonnes in 2014. Coffee grows in seven regions, namely West, Northwest, Littoral, Southwest, South, Centre, and East. Arabica is grown in the high plateau areas of Bamileke and Bamaoun with Robusta production predominantly in the other regions.

The Democratic Republic of the Congo was one of Africa's big coffee producers but declined to deficient levels. According to Knoema, a privately owned data platform based in the US, the DRC produced 54,089 tonnes in 2021, up from 53,303 tonnes the previous year. The DRC produces Arabica and Robusta varieties, and has had some exceptional coffee lots that scored high in the Taste of Harvest cupping conducted by the African Fine Coffees Association (AFCA). Most of the coffee is grown on the country's eastern side, with the biggest volume coming from the Kivu and the Ituri regions, along the Albertine Rift Valley, where the Lakes Kivu, Edward, and Albert lie. The country possesses suitable agro-climatic conditions, with high altitudes and volcanic soils favourable for Arabica. The DRC has a rich coffee heritage, but the industry has faced significant challenges in recent decades. Historically, the DRC was a major coffee producer, but years of political instability, armed conflict, and inadequate infrastructure have taken a toll on the industry. These challenges resulted in a decline in production and a loss of export markets. Efforts are underway to revive and develop the sector.

In recent years, there have been efforts to revitalise and rebuild the sector. Café Africa RDC has supported government efforts, with several local and international initiatives emerging to support farmers and improve the quality of the produce. These initiatives focus on training farmers in modern agricultural practices, providing access to finance and market linkages. The industry has great potential due to the country's diverse ecosystems, which contribute to unique flavours and profiles. Despite ongoing challenges such as limited access to credit, lack of infrastructure, and pests and diseases, there is growing interest and investment in the DRC's coffee sector. The government, international organisations, and local cooperatives are working together to address these issues and support the sustainable development of the coffee industry.

Malawi is a small, landlocked country in South-eastern Africa, with a population of about 20 million. Agriculture is the primary driver of the economy, supporting about 90% of the country's rural population, and coffee is one of the crops grown. The crop typically grows at an altitude between 3,000 and 8,000 feet (914 to 2,438 metres) above sea level. This varying altitude means that quality differs between estates. While famous for tobacco, Malawi is also known for some unique coffees. These may not be comparable to Kenyan or Ethiopian coffees, but typically the much higher quality coffees grow at higher elevations. Malawi has between 3,000 and 4,000 smallholder farmers organised into six cooperatives: Misuku, Phoko, Viphya North, Nkhatabay Highlands, South East Mzimba, and Ntchisi East. Malawi coffee has been made especially famous by the Mzuzu Coffee Planters

Cooperative Union, which brings together coffee farmers mainly from the Misuku hills.

The Mzuzu Union is a democratic cooperative body that empowers farmers in various ways. It supports their access to fair trade certification, thus opening opportunities for access to niche markets, which enables the union to support food security, good education and decent accommodation for the farmers. The Union ensures that farmers meet the customers' need for quality coffee, from which they obtain premiums that enable them to provide services to the growers.

The decline in Malawi's coffee sector has worried policy-makers. The country exported approximately 109,000 bags of 60 kilos of coffee in 1993, but 28 years on, the figure had dropped to about 9,000 bags a year. Discussions have been ongoing with development partners, including the World Bank, on addressing the challenges in the sector.

Jamaica, a Caribbean country, is renowned for producing high-quality coffee. Jamaica is famous for its Blue Mountain coffee, considered one of the world's finest and most sought-after coffees. The unique combination of high-altitude cultivation, rich volcanic soil, cool climate, and abundant rainfall in the Blue Mountains contributes to the coffee's distinctive flavour profile. Production primarily focuses on the island's eastern part, particularly in the Blue Mountains region. The industry is regulated by the Coffee Industry Board (CIB), which ensures quality control, grading, and marketing.

Jamaica has strict regulations to protect quality and integrity. Only coffee grown in specific areas of the Blue Mountains and meeting certain criteria can be labelled "Jamaican Blue Mountain Coffee." The CIB oversees the certification process and grants the use of the official seal to authorised producers. Due to its limited production volume and high demand, Jamaican Blue Mountain coffee is often priced at a premium. It is highly sought after by connoisseurs worldwide, contributing to its exclusivity and premium price.

The coffee industry faces some challenges, including fluctuations in weather patterns, climate change, pests and diseases, and labour availability. The government and industry stakeholders are working together to address these issues so as to ensure sustainability. Nevertheless, the country's coffee production is relatively small compared to other nations, with annual production averaging around 200,000 to 300,000 60-kilogram bags.

The limited production volume is partly due to the specific geographic and climatic conditions required for growing coffee in the Blue Mountains. The combination of high altitude, cool temperatures, abundant rainfall, and rich volcanic soil creates an ideal environment for specialty coffee cultivation. The Blue Mountain variety has a mild flavour, low acidity, and smooth taste, and is regarded as one of the world's finest and most expensive coffees. The small-scale production and reputation for exceptional quality contribute to its exclusivity and premium pricing. Due to the limited supply and high demand, Jamaican coffee is primarily exported to international markets, where connoisseurs and specialty coffee retailers greatly value it.

Papua New Guinea (PNG) has a notable coffee industry with a long history of production. Coffee is one of the country's major agricultural exports and an essential source of income for many smallholder farmers. According to Perfect Daily Grind, PNG ranks 17th in the world as a producer. The crop is grown by over 450,000 households in 18 of the 22 provinces. The annual production was around 752,000 bags in 2019, increasing to around 800,000 60-kg bags. Cultivation is primarily in the highland regions, particularly in the Eastern Highlands, Western Highlands, Simbu, and Morobe provinces. The country's diverse microclimates, volcanic soils, and high-altitude areas provide favourable conditions. Most production comes from smallholder farmers who cultivate on small plots of land. They typically employ traditional methods, including shade-grown coffee and organic practices. The coffee is often grown alongside other crops, promoting biodiversity and sustainable farming practices.

PNG is known for its unique coffee varieties, including the Arabica Typica and Bourbon, as well as some cultivars developed specifically for the region. The beans are usually hand-picked, and the cherries undergo wet processing to remove the pulp before drying. One notable aspect of the local industry is the presence of coffee cooperatives, which provide support and services to farmers, such as training, access to credit, and assistance with processing and marketing. Cooperatives help smallholder farmers collectively market their coffee and secure better prices. While PNG has significant potential for coffee production, the industry faces some challenges. Infrastructure limitations, including inadequate road networks and limited access to processing facilities, can affect the timely delivery of coffee from remote areas to markets. Additionally, fluctuating global prices, climate change, and pest and disease outbreaks can impact production and profitability. The Coffee Industry Corporation of Papua New Guinea (CIC) regulates the sector.

Conclusion

Coffee-producing countries are also increasingly becoming significant coffee consumers, owing to increasing urbanisation and middle-class growth. With this expansion, the value chain dynamics lead to increased economic opportunities, including job creation and better prices for the producers, with the potential of addressing poverty concerns among farmers. Recognising the potential to improve the livelihoods of producers, the ICO launched a programme to promote consumption in coffee-producing countries so as to take advantage of domestic market opportunities and stimulate value chain development. Hopefully, the trends of increased consumption in coffee-producing countries will lead to significant value chain developments and translate into better returns for producers. The next chapter discusses coffee culture in general.

6

Coffee as a Culture

There are different cultures associated with coffee among the producers and different cultures in the consuming countries. There is an elaborate coffee ceremony in Ethiopia, where the Arabica variety originated. In general, coffee can be described as a cultural phenomenon that goes beyond its culinary function as a beverage. There are several ways in which it can be seen as a part of the culture, including social rituals, cultural identity, art and literature, traditional practices and cultural exchange. In several African countries, the coffee culture served as a key ingredient in sealing blood covenants — common in Buganda and among the Banyakitara people of Western Uganda. It also has a significant economic impact on both producing and consuming communities, and its influence also manifests in many cultures through culinary experiences.

In many societies, the beverage is enjoyed as part of social rituals and gatherings, whether meeting friends at a café, sharing a cup with colleagues at work, or hosting coffee parties at home. In many settings, coffee provides a platform for social interactions and strengthens social bonds. It is deeply ingrained in the cultural identity of many countries and regions, playing significant roles in their history, traditions, and daily life. In addition to Ethiopia, countries like Uganda (particularly the Buganda kingdom), Colombia, and Brazil have rich coffee cultures that have shaped their heritage and are closely associated with national identities. Coffee has inspired artists, writers, and poets throughout history, being depicted in paintings, mentioned in various literature, and celebrated in music. Coffeehouses have historically served as gathering places for intellectuals and creatives, facilitating the exchange of ideas and topical discussions and being responsible for the birth of artistic movements.

In his book *Uncommon grounds: The history of coffee and how it transformed our world,* Mark Pendergrast narrates how coffee has been a vehicle for cultural exchange and globalisation. Pendergrast covers the politics around coffee, the various cultural conflicts associated with the crop and beverage, its trading, and its economic impact in various countries, from the Middle East to Asia, Europe and North America. Coffee culture is diverse, with distinctive highlights in the different countries — though **Ethiopia** stands out. As we can glean from various sources, we see that as cultivation and trade spread across the world, different cultures adopted their unique ways of preparing, serving, and enjoying coffee. Today, coffeehouses and cafes reflect diverse cultural influences and provide spaces for people from different backgrounds to unite. In some cultures, specific preparations or rituals have been passed down through generations. These traditions often involve unique brewing methods, ceremonies, or customs associated with coffee consumption. They serve as a way to connect with ancestral practices and preserve cultural heritage. Coffee is not just a drink; it has become a culinary experience.

Culture and Origins of the Discovery of Coffee

Though Arabica grew wild in Ethiopia (and still does) and Robusta too grew wild in the Lake Victoria basin and the equatorial rain forest belt of Central Africa, coffee played a central role in African cultural practices. It was critical in the unification of communities and in sealing blood covenants between tribes or warring factions that agreed to be at peace with each other. When it became a commercial crop, coffeebrought many people together in the quest for markets or better commercial prospects for members of village cooperatives or larger cooperative organisations.

In Ethiopia, it has been an important beverage for centuries, ever since it was discovered by Abyssinian monks around 850 AD. A goat herder, Kaldi, reportedly delivered the coffee beans to the monks after noticing their effects on his goats. Folklore holds that coffee cultivation began in Ethiopia around the ninth century. The legend of Kaldi, his goats and the monks says that coffee was discovered as a stimulant and beverage on the same day. However, according to historians, it is far more likely that coffee beans were chewed as a stimulant for centuries before they were made into a beverage.

Uganda is well known for its Robusta production and being its origin, though very little has been written or published about its origin in Eastern and Central African equatorial forests. As more of Uganda's Robusta is wet-processed, the profile is emerging of a rich aroma, a full chocolatey body typically with caramel and nutty notes, with low acidity and high caffeine content. The coffee culture in Uganda is centred around smallholder farmers, and ceremonies are sometimes conducted during special occasions or cultural events.

The Ethiopian Coffee Ceremony

I first encountered the Ethiopian coffee ceremony in 1996, on my first visit to Addis Ababa, the capital city, and I just loved it. I thought it was a great culture, and it is no wonder that Ethiopians drink most of the coffee they produce, compelling the government to put specific measures and restrictions to ensure that there is coffee for export. Otherwise, Ethiopians are perfectly capable of drinking all the coffee. I do not know of any other coffee-producing country with such a culture, but it is undoubtedly part of the pride of being Ethiopian and expressing how coffee is their gift to the world. They indeed enjoy the gift themselves, perhaps even more than those to whom they have bestowed it!

The Ethiopian ceremony is considered a symbol of hospitality, community, and friendship. Traditionally, it takes place in the host's home and is often performed by women skilled in the art of coffee preparation. The ceremony can be a formal or informal gathering, depending on the occasion and the number of guests, and due to modern variations, it can take place at various public functions, but there always has to be a host.

The host begins by washing green coffee, often in front of the guests, to demonstrate the use of fresh, unroasted beans. These are then roasted in a pan over an open fire or charcoal stove, releasing their aromatic flavours. Freshly roasted, they are then ground using a mortar and pestle or a traditional coffee grinder known as a *mukecha.* The process is by hand, and the grinding is carefully done to achieve the desired consistency. The ground product is placed in a traditional clay coffee pot called a *jebena,* along with water. The jebena is heated on a charcoal stove or open fire, allowing the coffee to brew slowly. As it brews, a fragrant aroma fills the room. The host uses a long-necked spouted pot, called a *finjal,* to pour the brew into small cups called "cini" or "sini." The coffee is poured from a height to create a frothy layer on top. The cups are often placed on a decorative tray along with small snacks, typically 'kolo' (a mixture of roasted barley and peanuts) or popcorn to accompany the beverage.

The coffee is served starting with the eldest or most honoured guest. It is customary to have three rounds of coffee, with each offering having a different flavour profile—strong, medium, and weak. Guests are encouraged to savour the beverage, engage in conversation, and enjoy the company of others. The Ethiopian ceremony is more than just a means of preparing and serving coffee; it is a social ritual that brings people together, fosters community bonds, and celebrates Ethiopian cultural heritage.

The Buganda Coffee Culture and Ceremony

The Baganda people of Uganda have their own unique coffee ceremony, which used to be an important part of their cultural heritage and social gatherings. Unfortunately, many people are ignorant of it because social upheavals caused the loss of much of the heritage.

Long before the arrival of the first Europeans in Buganda (part of modern-day Uganda) in the late 1800s, the Baganda had Robusta coffee growing wild in the forests or bushes, and some of that found its way into their gardens. The Buganda coffee customs date back to the 15th Century AD, and at some point in history, it was part of barter trade, where it served as a pseudo currency.

In social interactions, the coffee bean had great significance in fostering cordial relations among the Baganda. just like the kola nut in some West African cultures. A visitor would be welcomed with a coffee pack (called *ettu ly'emmwanyi*), which was ripe coffee cherries steamed in banana leaves and dried over the fireplace. Before steaming, the cherries were wrapped in banana fibres and dried over the fireplace, giving the coffee a unique flavour.

The visitor would be treated to this coffee and served some cool drinking water from a clay pot to quench their thirst. The coffee beans were also perhaps chewed as a stimulant. This ceremony was significant as a symbol of hospitality, tradition, and communal bonding. During the traditional marriage ceremony, there is usually a time to chew some coffee beans, as a significant aspect of Kiganda culture.

The Baganda also had a ceremony known as *Okutt'omukago,* which was a blood covenant where two parties exchanged coffee beans, where a slight incision was made at the navel of each of the concerned individuals, and a coffee bean was smeared with a drop of blood by the two covenanting parties. They then exchanged the beans as a sign of the covenant. This was common among high-profile personalities, like between the Buganda king and another king or between chiefs and other figures of social standing, as a sign of peace, brotherhood, or commitment to each other.

There was another more elaborate ceremony, similar to the Ethiopian one, but not quite as complex. The king of Buganda, also known as the Kabaka, had close ties with the Emperor of Ethiopia, and it is likely that the Ethiopian sovereign influenced the Buganda ceremony. Suffice it to say the Buganda tradition has largely been lost. It typically used to take place in a designated area, often outdoors, where a mat or grass was spread. It now is, admittedly, rarely seen, but needs to be revived to promote domestic coffee consumption. The mother in the home would normally prepare for the ceremony by drying the cherries and having the husks taken off through *rough hulling* (normally with a pestle and a mortar). The fresh beans would then be roasted over a charcoal stove or open fire, and carefully monitored and roasted to achieve the desired roast level. Once roasted, they would then be ground using a traditional mortar and pestle (but a manual grinder, known as *olubengo*, could be used to get the finer powder). The ground coffee would then be placed in a metallic coffee pot known as *ebbinika*, and water is added to the pot, and the mixture then heated over a fire or stove until it reached a boiling point. When I was young and lived in the countryside, I participated in this ceremony, but I must admit that I have never seen it in any urban setting in Buganda.

Before serving the coffee, the host would perform a series of rituals, such as offering prayers or pouring a small amount of coffee onto the ground as an offering to ancestors. This libation was a common practice, but with the advent of Christianity, the connotation of communicating with ancestors was considered satanic, and communities began to shun the practice. In the home where I grew up, whatever the circumstances, my father did not permit libation practices or ancestral worship.

After this preparation, the brew was then poured into small cups, often made of pottery or gourds. The mother or a designated person served the coffee to the guests, starting with the eldest or most respected individuals. It was customary that as the coffee was poured, the guests savoured the rich flavours while engaging in conversations and storytelling. Storytelling was significant in the Kiganda culture, with grandparents narrating historical events.

The Baganda ceremony holds cultural significance beyond the preparation and consumption of coffee. The ceremony honoured guests, showed hospitality and strengthened community ties. Where there is a big gathering, the ceremony may include traditional music and dance, further enhancing the cultural experience. It reflects the Baganda people's deep appreciation for coffee as a cherished beverage and their commitment to preserving their cultural heritage. It served as an event that fostered unity, storytelling, and the passing down of traditions from one generation to the next. Nonetheless, as mentioned earlier, Uganda's social and political upheavals disrupted some cultural practices, the coffee ceremony significantly so, as it has practically died out with the passing of the older generations.

The Robusta Coffee Link with Africa

While the Baganda had coffee as part of their culture for centuries before the European explorers came to the continent, it did not become a commercial crop in Uganda until the turn of the 19th Century when the British introduced Arabica coffee. British agriculturalists set up a botanic garden in Entebbe (presently a conservation area) where they experimented with various crops, including coffee from Malawi (then known as Nyasaland, en route from Ethiopia). From the research in Entebbe, Arabica seedlings were taken to various areas to set up coffee estates beginning in central Uganda, where the Baganda were employed as labourers on the farms. The Arabica was subsequently planted in the Mount Elgon area in the east, the Mountains of the Moon in the west of the country, and the West Nile region. The people in the central region realised that the crop now planted on a commercial scale had similarities to the coffee bushes they had in their gardens. Thus, the Baganda started to plant more of those bushes around their homes, given that the white settlers seemed to like the cherries. At this time, the British had yet to engage in the scientific identification of Robusta coffee.

The discovery of Robusta coffee, scientifically known as *Coffea canephora*, did not have a legendary dramatic story like that of Arabica coffee. Robusta was known to indigenous populations, like the Baganda, and in the regions where it grew naturally in the Lake Victoria basin and the equatorial forests of the area known as the Great Lakes region of Eastern and Central Africa. Uganda was the epicentre of the origin of Robusta, which still grows wild in the Kibale forest of Western Uganda, the Zoka forest in the West Nile region, and the forested areas near the border with the Democratic Republic of Congo.

Scientifically, Robusta was first recognised as a distinct coffee species in the late 19th century by French botanist and explorer Antoine Chevalier. In 1897, Chevalier encountered Robusta plants growing in the Congo Basin during a botanical expedition. He took samples back to France, where they were studied and classified as a separate coffee species. The name "Robusta" was given to this species because of its robust nature and ability to thrive in various environments, including lower altitudes and regions with less favourable conditions than Arabica. The point to note here is that this coffee was already part and parcel of the Buganda culture for centuries. While Robusta is known for its higher caffeine content, resistance to pests and diseases, and its characteristic strong and bitter flavour profile, Uganda's is unique because it naturally grows at relatively high latitudes (between 1,000 metres and 1,300 metres). Thus, it has relatively *mild* characteristics and compares favourably with some Arabica varieties when processed through the wet method.

Unlike the legend surrounding the discovery of Arabica, the story of the discovery of Robusta is based on botanical exploration and scientific classification. However, Robusta has played a significant role in the global coffee industry, particularly in the manufacture of instant coffee and espresso blends due to its affordability and characteristics that complement specific taste preferences and manufacturing processes.

Coffee Cultures in Other African Countries

Apart from Ethiopia and Uganda, several African countries with notable coffee cultures deserve recognition. They are not big producers but are known for their coffee production and unique cultures. We will examine Cameroon, DR Congo, Kenya, Tanzania and Rwanda.

Cameroon does not have a specific cultural ceremony associated with coffee. However, coffee holds cultural and economic importance in Cameroon, and specific customs and traditions are related to its production and consumption. The crop is primarily grown in the western regions and is a significant export produce. While there is no formal ceremony, there are cultural practices and traditions: in some rural communities, traditional methods of preparing coffee are still practised, which may involve roasting the beans over an open fire, grinding them manually using a mortar and pestle, and brewing the beverage in a pot or using a cloth filter to sieve out the grinds while pouring boiling water over the ground coffee. Sharing a cup of coffee is often a part of social interactions and gatherings as domestic consumption increases. It is common for friends, family, or guests to be offered a cup as a gesture of hospitality and to foster conversation and bonding. Over the last 10 years, a ceremony known as *Festicoffee* has rallied Cameroonians to drink coffee and celebrate what the country produces.

Coffee plays a role in cultural celebrations and ceremonies such as weddings, funerals, and traditional festivals. It may be served as a part of the hospitality offered to the guests, symbolising warmth and community. Regarding its economic impact, coffee is an important cash crop for many smallholder farmers. The industry contributes to the economy and provides livelihoods for numerous individuals and communities involved in cultivation, processing, and trade. While there may not be a formal ceremony, it is vital to acknowledge the cultural practices and traditions surrounding coffee, which reflect its significance in daily life, social interactions, and cultural events. Coffee represents a connection to the land, a source of income, and a symbol of hospitality and togetherness.

Kenya is renowned for producing high-quality specialty coffee. The Kenyan produce is known for its bright acidity, fruity flavours, and distinctive profiles. The coffee culture revolves around smallholder farms, cooperative systems, and auctions that promote transparency and quality. Coffeehouses serve as social hubs. The Mount Kenya area is where the bulk, 70%, of the coffee is grown. The locals have a coffee ceremony, a social event where people drink coffee and discuss various issues. Also, unknown to many Kenyans, due to its presence mainly in some coastal communities, there is another cultural ceremony associated with coffee known as *Kahawa Chungu* ceremony. It is a traditional coffee preparation and serving ritual that holds cultural significance, particularly among the Giriama and Pokomo people who are part of the nine ethnic groups that comprise the Mijikenda people who inhabit the Kenyan coast.

Kahawa Chungu means "bitter coffee" in the Swahili language. It is often drunk by older men and is believed to have an aphrodisiac effect. It typically takes place during special occasions, gatherings, or as a welcoming gesture for guests. The ceremony begins with the roasting of the coffee beans on a hot metal plate or pan over an open fire. This process is accompanied by the aroma of the roasting beans, creating a sensory experience. After the beans are roasted, they are ground using a mortar and pestle. This traditional grinding method is performed manually, producing a coarse coffee grind. The ground powder is then brewed using a traditional clay or metal coffee pot called a *jebena*. It is brewed slowly over a charcoal stove or open fire. This method allows the flavours and aromas to develop fully. Once the coffee is ready, it is poured into small traditional cups. The host or hostess serves the coffee to guests, starting with the elders or special guests. It is customary to serve three rounds of coffee, each with a distinct flavour: the first round is strong, the second is medium, and the third is weak. The Kenyan coffee ceremony emphasises hospitality and togetherness. It provides an opportunity for gathering, conversation, and strengthening social bonds. The host or hostess takes pride in serving and ensuring guests are comfortable and well cared for.

It is a way to celebrate and showcase the country's rich coffee culture, flavours, and hospitality. While the ceremonies are not widespread and may vary across different Kenyan communities, the essence of sharing and appreciating coffee remains a common thread. They are now being enhanced or modified by the modern café, which are mushrooming in urban centres. For many years, the Kenya Coffee Safari was an excursion that offered visitors opportunities to visit farmers and experience the culture at its origin, which helped many appreciate Kenyan coffee even more.

Tanzania is another African country with a rich coffee heritage. It produces Arabica and Robusta, with the latter being the most prominent. Tanzanian coffee is known for its medium to full body, bright acidity, and fruity or floral flavours. In regions like Kilimanjaro and Arusha, coffee tours and visits to farms offer insights into the production process and the cultural significance. Tanzania has a cultural ceremony called *Kahawa Tungu*, an important cultural tradition, particularly among the Chagga and Haya ethnic groups who reside in the coffee-growing regions such as the slopes of Mount Kilimanjaro and the southern highlands. The occasion is a ceremonial coffee preparation and serving ritual that typically occurs during social gatherings, special events, or as a symbol of hospitality. Here is an overview of the ceremony.

The ceremony begins with the roasting of green coffee beans in a shallow pan or skillet over an open fire. The aroma fills the air, creating a sensory experience. The beans are then ground using a mortar and pestle or a manual grinder. The grinding is often done by hand, resulting in a coarse coffee which is then brewed using a traditional clay or metal coffee pot called a *jebena* or *dallah*. The coffee is typically brewed slowly over a charcoal stove or open fire. The slow brewing allows the flavours to develop fully. Once the coffee is ready, it is poured into small cups known as *kikombe cha kahawa* (coffee cup) or *tungu*. The host or hostess serves the guests, starting with the elders or special guests. It is customary to serve three rounds, each with a distinct flavour strength: the first round is strong, the second is medium, and the third is weak. The Tanzanian ceremony is not only about serving coffee but also about hospitality, community, and cultural exchange. It provides an opportunity for people to come together, share stories, and strengthen social bonds. The host or hostess takes pride in preparing and serving coffee while ensuring the guests are comfortable and well taken care of in a cultural expression of the importance of coffee in Tanzanian society, particularly in the regions where coffee is grown. It serves as a way to celebrate Tanzanian coffee, showcase the country's cultural heritage, and foster a sense of togetherness among community members and visitors.

The coastal people of Tanzania - Zanzibar, Dar es Salaam, and the surrounding areas - particularly the Swahili community, have a special ceremony known as the "Swahili Coffee Ceremony" or *Kahawa ya Uswahilini.* It is an important social and cultural event that typically occurs during special occasions, festive gatherings, or as a gesture of hospitality. The ceremony begins with the roasting of green beans in a pan or skillet over an open fire or stove. The aroma fills the air as the beans roast, creating a delightful atmosphere. The beans are ground using a manual grinder or mortar and pestle in a process that produces a coarse coffee grind, which is preferred in Swahili coffee preparation. Ground coffee is brewed using a traditional clay or metal coffee pot called a *jebena* or *dallah.* The coffee is typically brewed slowly over a charcoal or wood fire. The brewing allows the flavours to develop fully, resulting in a flavourful and aromatic coffee. The brew is served in small cups or decorative coffee pots. The host or hostess pours the coffee into the cups, starting with the elders or special guests. Serving multiple rounds of coffee is customary, allowing guests to savour different strengths and flavours.

The Swahili ceremony is not just about the coffee but also about socialising, hospitality, and cultural exchange. It provides an opportunity for family members, friends, and neighbours to come together, engage in conversations, and strengthen community bonds. The ceremony is often accompanied by traditional music, dance, and storytelling, adding to the festive ambience.

The Democratic Republic of Congo (DRC) is known for its unique coffees, in spite of the political and social instability of many decades. Its production is centred in the Lake Kivu provinces, where about 11,000 farmers cultivate both Robusta and Arabica. The coffee-growing regions like the Ubangi of Northwest DRC have a ceremony in which the serving of coffee occurs during social gatherings, celebrations, or as a gesture of hospitality. While the specific details may vary across different regions and communities, it begins with roasting green beans in a pan or skillet over an open fire. The roasting is accompanied by the aroma of the beans, creating a sensory experience. After roasting, the coffee beans are ground manually using a mortar, pestle, or grinder, producing a coarse coffee grind that preserves the flavours and aromas. The brewing uses a traditional clay or metal coffee pot, slowly over a charcoal stove or open fire, allowing the flavours to develop fully. The brewing may involve multiple rounds to achieve the desired strength and flavour. Once the coffee is brewed, it is served in small cups or bowls. The host or hostess takes pride in serving, often starting with the elders or special guests. It is common to serve multiple rounds of coffee, each with varying strength.

The Congolese ceremony is not only about preparing and serving coffee but also about hospitality and community. It allows people to come together, engage in conversations, and strengthen social bonds. The ceremony may be accompanied by traditional songs, dances, or storytelling, creating a festive and communal atmosphere. It celebrates the cultural significance of coffee and reflects the country's rich heritage and traditions. While the ceremony may differ in specific details across regions and communities, it serves as a way to honour guests, foster connections, and highlight the importance of coffee in Congolese culture.

Rwandan coffee is known for its bright acidity, floral aromas, and complex flavours. The country's industry has experienced significant growth and recognition in recent years. The nation has embraced coffee as a tool for economic development and poverty alleviation, and initiatives such as the Rwandan Coffee Festival celebrate the coffee culture and promote coffee tourism. Rwanda celebrates *coffee days* when the National Agricultural Exports Development Board (NAEB), in partnership with other stakeholders, prepares the Rwanda Coffee Day when there is interaction with farmers, mainly for them to taste the beverage that results from their produce. The country has not had a history of coffee culture and, by the early 2020s, effort was being made to enlighten the farmers (most of whom get to taste coffee for the first time) and train them in coffee preparation at home using available traditional means for roasting and grinding. This ceremony is becoming an important part of Rwandan culture.

Burundi, a neighbour to Rwanda, very similar culturally and in topography, is a small landlocked country with a burgeoning coffee industry. Cultivation is a vital income source for many rural Burundi communities. Burundian coffee is often characterised by its wine-like acidity, fruity flavours, and delicate profiles. Coffee washing stations play a crucial role in the value chain, and coffee cupping sessions and tastings provide opportunities to explore the country's offerings. Burundi has a cultural ceremony, a traditional coffee preparation and serving ritual that holds cultural significance in the society.

The ceremony is often performed during social gatherings, celebrations, or as a symbol of hospitality. It begins with the roasting of green beans in a pan or skillet over an open fire. As the beans roast, they release a fragrant aroma, creating an enticing atmosphere. They are then ground using a mortar and pestle or a manual grinder, which produces a coarse coffee grind, preserving the flavours and aromas. The ground coffee is brewed using a traditional clay or metal coffee pot known as a *cagoré* or *kanzima*. The brewing is slow over a charcoal or wood fire, and it allows the flavours to develop fully, resulting in a rich and flavourful cup of coffee. The brew is served in small cups known as *ikaré* or *inapa*. The host or hostess serves the coffee to guests, starting with the elders or special guests. Serving multiple rounds of coffee is customary, allowing guests to enjoy different strengths and flavours.

The Burundian ceremony is not just about preparing and serving coffee but also about hospitality, community, and cultural traditions. It provides an opportunity for people to come together, engage in conversations, and strengthen social bonds. It may include traditional songs, dances, or storytelling, creating a joyful and festive atmosphere. It serves as a way to celebrate special occasions, foster connections, and honour guests through the sharing of coffee and cultural traditions.

Ghana, though much more known for cocoa production, also produces coffee and there is an associated cultural ceremony. It is a traditional coffee preparation and serving ritual that holds cultural significance in certain Ghanaian communities, particularly among the Akan people. The ceremony is typically performed in social gatherings, family events, or as a symbol of hospitality. It begins with the roasting of green beans in a pan or skillet over an open fire. As the beans roast, they release an inviting aroma, creating a sensory experience. They are then ground using a manual grinder or mortar and pestle. The process produces a coarse coffee grind that maintains flavours and characteristics; it is then brewed using a traditional clay or metal coffee pot. The coffee is typically brewed slowly over a charcoal stove or open fire. The brewing process allows the flavours to develop fully, resulting in a rich and aromatic offering which is then served in small cups or calabash bowls. The host or hostess serves the coffee to guests, starting with the elders or special guests. It is customary to serve multiple rounds of coffee, each with varying strength or sweetness based on individual preferences.

The Ghanaian ceremony emphasises hospitality, community, and cultural exchange. It provides an opportunity for people to come together, engage in conversations, and strengthen social bonds. The ceremony is often accompanied by traditional songs, dances, or storytelling, creating a festive and joyful atmosphere. The ceremony represents the cultural significance of coffee in Ghanaian society, particularly among the Akan, and serves as a way to showcase the country's cultural heritage, and demonstrate the warm hospitality for which Ghanaians are known.

The different African countries highlighted above represent just a fraction of the diverse coffee cultures found across the continent. Each country has its unique coffee production methods, flavour profiles, and cultural traditions surrounding the crop and its beverage. Exploring these cultures can provide a deeper understanding of the rich heritage and the impact of coffee on the livelihoods of farmers and communities.

Coffee and Culture in Latin America

Although coffee originates in Africa, Latin America is the largest producer region in the world, accounting for almost 60% of global exports. Mexico is included in this group as part of Latin America, despite being the only North American country that is part of Latin America. Mexico is one of the region's largest countries, a recognised and significant producer. Latin American countries do not have specific traditional coffee ceremonies as elaborate and formalised as those in countries like Ethiopia or Yemen. However, coffee holds great cultural significance in many countries, and certain customs and traditions are associated with coffee preparation and consumption. I will examine Mexico, Guatemala, Costa Rica, Brazil, and Colombia. While these countries may not have formal ceremonies, their coffee cultures and traditions are rooted in the appreciation and enjoyment of the beverage. Each country has its unique customs, brewing methods, and coffee rituals, reflecting the cultural significance of this beloved beverage in the region.

Mexico has a rich coffee culture though it may not have a ceremony. It has several coffee-related traditions, with coffee often prepared and enjoyed as part of everyday life, whether at home, cafes, or social gatherings. Mexicans have unique ways, but these practices are more informal and less ceremonial than the structured ceremonies in other cultures. Mexican coffee traditions often revolve around the popular brewing method called *Café de Olla*. *Café de Olla* is a traditional Mexican preparation that involves brewing coffee with cinnamon, piloncillo (a type of unrefined cane sugar), and sometimes other spices. This method imparts a distinctive flavour profile to the coffee, giving it a sweet and aromatic taste.

For many Mexicans, sharing a cup with friends, family, or colleagues is essential to hospitality and social interactions. They often engage in conversations, storytelling, or business meetings while enjoying a cup of coffee. Regions like Chiapas, Veracruz, Oaxaca, and Puebla are known for their cultivation and are home to various coffee estates and cooperatives. Exploring the local culture and visiting coffee farms or cooperatives can provide insights into the traditional aspects of Mexican coffee production and appreciation.

Guatemala, ***Mexico***, ***Honduras*** and ***Peru*** are significant players as well. While Guatemala does not have a formal ceremony, local households often have a designated time in the morning or after meals to gather and enjoy coffee together. It is typically brewed using traditional methods such as a cloth filter called a *filtro*, and it is common to serve the beverage alongside traditional Guatemalan sweet breads or pastries.

Costa Rica is not a big producer country but is known for its high-quality. Local preparation is often brewed using a traditional drip brewer known as a *chorreador*. The process involves pouring hot water over a cloth filter filled with coffee grounds, allowing the coffee to drip into a pot or cup. This method is considered a part of the country's coffee culture and heritage.

Brazil, the largest coffee-producing country in the world, has a strong culture but does not have a specific traditional coffee ceremony like the elaborate ceremonies in some other countries. Nevertheless, coffee holds significant cultural and historical importance. The culture is more focused on cultivation, production, and consumption than formal ceremonies. There are customs and traditions, nevertheless, that include Cafézinho, which means "little coffee" in Portuguese, a common term that describes a small cup of black coffee, served as a gesture of hospitality in homes, offices, and businesses. Visitors are offered a cup of cafézinho upon arrival as a way to welcome them and create a warm atmosphere.

Coffee is an integral part of breakfast in Brazil, typically served alongside bread, cheese, or other typical breakfast items. Many Brazilians enjoy a cup after meals as a digestive aid and to prolong the dining experience. The country has many variations, including the popular *cafezinho*, *cafezinho com leite* (coffee with milk), *pingado* (espresso with a dash of milk), *cafezinho coado* (filtered coffee) and *carioca* — which is a lighter coffee — where they add more water to the brew. These variations cater to different tastes and preferences. In workplaces and educational institutions, coffee breaks are common, and provide an opportunity for people to take a short break, socialise, and enjoy a cup. Moreover, coffee breaks are often seen as a way to relax and recharge during the day.

For those who have visited Brazil, an important part of the cultural experience is the plantation tours, which help visitors to appreciate the Brazilian coffee industry. Production is concentrated in regions like Minas Gerais, São Paulo, and Espírito Santo, and visitors can often take tours of plantations, known as *fazendas*, to learn about cultivation, participate in tastings, and gain insights into the industry. Exploring the coffee regions, enjoying different variations, and experiencing the hospitality associated with coffee can provide a rich and immersive experience; and so, even though Brazil may not have a formal ceremony, something about coffee is deeply embedded in the country's culture and daily life.

Colombia does not have a specific traditional ceremony like the elaborate ones found in Ethiopia. Nevertheless, the crop plays a central role in local culture, and specific customs and traditions are associated with preparing and enjoying the beverage. Coffee is deeply ingrained in daily life, and Colombians take pride in their heritage. Customs and traditions include *La Hora del Café* (Coffee Hour) where, in households, it is common to have designated times during the day, such as in the morning or after lunch, to gather and enjoy a cup together. This informal gathering often involves conversations, storytelling, or simply sharing quality time with family and friends while savouring the brew. Another is *tinto* and *Tinto Time: tinto* is the term used to refer to black coffee. It is a staple in local culture and can be enjoyed throughout the day. Many Colombians have a routine of taking a break during the day for a *tinto time*, where they pause their activities to enjoy a small cup of black coffee.

Colombia farms and scenic landscapes where coffee is cultivated are an attraction. Visitors often have the opportunity to tour coffee farms, learn about the production process, and experience tastings, gaining insights into the cultural significance of the beverage and appreciating the country's coffee heritage. Festivals are held in different regions. The most famous one is the National Coffee Festival (Festival Nacional del Café), which takes place in the Coffee Triangle region. The festivals feature parades, music, dance, coffee-tasting events, and competitions, highlighting the crop's cultural importance. Thus, while the country may not have a formal ceremony, its culture and traditions reflect the deep appreciation for the beverage and its role in society. Colombian coffee is renowned worldwide for its high quality, and experiencing the local coffee culture firsthand can provide a rich and immersive experience.

Coffee Cultures in Asia

While coffee ceremonies are more commonly associated with African countries like Ethiopia and Eritrea, there is one Asian country that has a traditional ritual: Japan. This East Asian country has a unique and formalised brewing method called "siphon coffee" or "vacuum coffee", which involves using a siphon pot consisting of two chambers connected by a tube. The water is heated in the lower chamber, and as the pressure increases, it rises to the upper one where it mixes with coffee grounds. After a specified brewing time, the heat source is removed, and the brewed coffee returns to the lower chamber through a filter. Although not specifically referred to as a ceremony, the process of preparing and serving siphon coffee has a ceremonial aspect to it.

The brewing is often done in front of the customers, showcasing precision, attention to detail, and a focus on aesthetics. The barista's skill in controlling variables such as water temperature, brew time, and extraction plays a significant role in the final flavour. The emphasis on precision, artistry, and the experience of watching the brewing process creates a unique culture that can be likened to a ceremonial practice. While it may not be as elaborate or culturally embedded as traditional ceremonies in other parts of the world, Japan's siphon brewing method offers a ceremony-like experience for coffee enthusiasts and a chance to appreciate the craftsmanship involved in preparing a cup of the beverage.

Asian Coffee Culture Highlights

Until recently, the biggest consumption in Asia was reportedly in Indonesia (but has been supplanted by China). Coffee has become a favourite beverage, thanks to promotion, investment in consumer needs identification, and the presentation of coffee in appealing ways. With a large youthful population, it was critical to make the beverage appealing to young professionals and students. A strategy was developed to target each market segment specifically. Thus, the promotion of coffee among the younger generation of Indonesians led to a significant increase in consumption that placed the country in Asia's high consumers league. Cultures in Asian coffee-producing countries vary based on local traditions, consumption habits, and historical influences. Below is an overview of the coffee cultures in other Asian producer countries.

China has an emerging coffee culture, with consumption on the rise, particularly in urban areas. Coffee shops, including international chains and local brands, are popular gathering places. The culture blends traditional tea culture with modern coffee trends, resulting in unique offerings like tea-infused coffee drinks.

Indonesia has a vibrant culture with a strong emphasis on specialty coffee. Traditional brewing methods such as *kopi tubruk* (direct brewing), *kopi susu* (coffee with condensed milk) are popular. Another, *kopi aren* (with palm sugar), was innovated by one of the coffee shops and became extremely popular when the President of Indonesia visited and ordered a cup. The country is known for its unique varieties, including Sumatra Mandheling, Gayo, Java Preanger, and Bali Kintamani.

Vietnam, Asia's biggest producer, has seen its consumption grow over the two decades to 2020, owing to the development of a new coffee culture. Coffee is deeply ingrained in Vietnamese culture, and the country is famous for its distinctive style known as *cà phê den đá* (iced coffee) and *cà phê sua đá* (iced coffee with condensed milk). It involves using a phin filter to brew a strong cup, which is then poured over ice and often enjoyed with sweetened condensed milk.

Thailand has a burgeoning scene, with an emphasis on specialty coffee and third-wave coffee culture in urban areas. Thai iced coffee, *oliang*, is a popular beverage made by mixing the brew with various spices and serving it over ice.

Myanmar (formerly known as Burma) has a growing culture, with a focus on specialty coffee. Traditional methods like *la phet yay* involve brewing coffee with condensed milk and serving it hot or iced. The country's unique varieties, such as Shan State coffee, are gaining recognition.

India's coffee culture and consumption patterns vary across the different regions. In the southern states of Karnataka, Kerala, and Tamil Nadu, where the crop is primarily grown, filter coffee is popular. It is made using a traditional metal filter and served with hot milk. In other parts of the country, instant coffee and espresso-based drinks are more common.

The Philippines has a strong culture, and local coffee shops called *kapehan* can be found throughout the country. Traditional Filipino coffee, known as *kapeng barako*, is brewed using a stovetop coffee maker called a *barako* pot. Filipino iced coffee, known as *sikwate*, is also enjoyed.

Malaysia has traditional coffee shops known as *kopitiams* which are an integral part of the culture. The popular beverage *kopi* is a strong, sweetened cup made with a sock-like filter called a "sock-brewer." Malaysians also enjoy iced versions, including *kopi ais* and *kopi peng*.

These descriptions provide a general overview of the coffee cultures in the different Asian coffee-producing countries. It is essential to note that coffee consumption and culture may significantly vary within each country, influenced by regional preferences, urbanisation, and globalisation. The continent's big population and the emerging consumption trends provide an excellent opportunity to develop a new culture around coffee.

Conclusion

Coffee production and trade have shaped many economies, creating jobs, influencing agricultural practices, and contributing to the overall development. The industry, from farmers to exporters and baristas, is a significant part of the economic fabric, and its cultural significance lies in its role as a social lubricant, a symbol of identity and heritage, an inspiration for artistic expression as a medium for cultural exchange. It embodies traditions, rituals, and social practices that contribute to culture. The next chapter discusses the World Coffee Producers' Forum. This initiative brings together producers worldwide and examines different efforts, as well as their failures, to address global poverty among coffee farmers, hence the formation of the global platform to have a continuing advocacy voice on this matter.

7

The World Coffee Producers Forum (WCPF)

The World Coffee Producers Forum is an international platform that brings together producers to discuss challenges, share knowledge, and work towards the sustainable development of the sector. The WCPF is a platform to collaborate, network and work with other industry stakeholders, including buyers, roasters, traders, policymakers, and researchers. It is becoming an important player on the global scene.

The forum facilitates the exchange of ideas, experiences, and best practices, and offers educational and informational sessions where participants can learn about various production, processing, marketing, and sustainability. Experts and industry leaders present research findings, case studies, and innovative solutions to address challenges faced by producers. Alarmed by the plight of farmers in all producer nations, with no end in sight to the suffering, representatives of coffee-producing countries met in Addis Ababa, Ethiopia, in 2016 and formed an alliance that came to be known as the WCPF. The new platform agreed to convene a global meeting every two years, with the first two hosted in 2017 and 2019 by Colombia and Brazil, respectively.

The First WCPF Global Meeting

The WCPF held its first global meeting in July 2017 in Medellín, Colombia, and had several dignitaries, including heads of state and representatives from more than 40 coffee-producing countries. Sessions covered topics such as climate change, sustainability of production and the challenge of prices that are non-remunerative to producers. The forum noted with concern that the crop is primarily produced by smallholder farmers, with a significant social and economic impact on large rural communities.

Coffee is no longer associated with prosperity in many producing countries, as used to be the case. It is actually increasingly linked to poverty in many communities. The WCPF noted a serious disconnect between the profit margins on the consumer and producer sides, often expressed as concern for the trade imbalance or unfair trade. At the outset, WCPF desired to explore ways to increase producers' incomes and, ultimately, alleviate poverty in rural areas of producer countries, some of which are also the world's poorest. While climate change was a key concern, more emphasis was put on farmers' economic sustainability, which came out strongly in the keynote address by Professor Jeffrey Sachs, a world-renowned economics professor, bestselling author, innovative educator, and global leader in sustainable development.

Participants echoed the need for the economic sustenance of producers as imperative for the sustainability of the global coffee industry. The forum discussed climate change and the resultant loss of biodiversity, and it was noted that addressing social and economic sustainability of producers could stimulate better environmental stewardship and contribute to environmental sustainability. It was noted that reducing plastic waste and other pollutants is critical throughout the coffee value chain, which needs the commitment of all actors.

The coordinators engaged Prof Sachs to research the entire value chain and propose solutions for the sustainability of the global industry. An official communication to the International Coffee Organization (ICO) requested the Executive Director to use the ICO's convening power to get the trade and industry to take the producers' plight seriously and develop solutions to address producers' poverty. The ICO subsequently pledged to be a mediator between producers and consumers.

The Second WCPF Global Meeting

The second WCPF global meeting took place in Campinas, Brazil in July 2019, and Prof Sachs presented a report from the study conducted by his team at Columbia University. His report was titled "Economic and Political Analysis to Improve Small Coffee Growers' Income". He outlined how producer countries struggled to achieve better productivity and that only Brazil and Vietnam had consistently risen in productivity where yields per hectare were excellent. He expressed concern that the other countries with lower productivity were likely to be squeezed. Prof Sachs noted that with the increased costs of production, there was a need for more productivity to assure the sustainability of the global value chain. To ramp up productivity, the Columbia University academic argued for the provision of improved coffee cultivars (planting materials such as better seedlings), improved agricultural practices, and better usage of inputs and funding for them all. He called for better information about the market, improved agricultural risk management, and better scientific research and development in agriculture. He also made a strong case for a global coffee fund of about 10 billion US dollars to address the cause of producer sustainability to ensure the achievement of the UN's Sustainable Development Goals (SDGs).

The Forum received reports from different countries highlighting achievements in promoting good agricultural practices and coffee consumption in the domestic markets. However, while the first Forum had raised worldwide awareness of the need for economic sustainability in global supply, it was noted that there was a lack of effective engagement from the other sectors in the value chain to effectively work on the improvement of producers' earnings. Prof Sachs flagged the need for global actions through an engagement and interaction of all agents in the value chain, in addition to those already carried out in each country.

The Second Forum made the following resolutions:

To promote the creation of a technological platform to aggregate and make available information and numbers to all segments of the value chain in a manner that creates transparency in business and price formulation.

To develop a mechanism that facilitates the availability of information from producing origins through traceability of offered products and their specificities to end consumers.

To promote the training of producers through technical assistance and rural extension for professionalisation in property management and acquiring knowledge about market risks.

The London Declaration

The build-up from the first and second WCPF global meetings led to an appeal to the global coffee companies to consider the plight of producers seriously and indicate what actions they intended to take. The companies were asked to consider candidly discussing with the ICO as the neutral convener. Subsequently, the global companies indicated their willingness to the ICO to participate in a dialogue with the producers under the auspices of the ICO, thus the convening of the 1st CEO and Global Leaders Forum, held on 23rd September 2019, where the London Declaration was signed by private sector companies and organisations. The parties acknowledged the impact of the coffee price crisis and expressed their commitment to continue the coffee sector dialogue with the aim of achieving solutions that are long-term and transformational.

The International Coffee Council (the ICO's apex body), noted the commitment of the ICO member countries to work together with the signatories of the London Declaration and other stakeholders in pursuit of the Sustainable Development Goals (SDGs). The parties were to jointly define detailed and concrete actions. The Council advised the ICO exporting and importing members to engage their national stakeholders to define their specific needs and priorities in discussing the London Declaration, in the pursuit of the collective commitment to a sustainable coffee sector. The Coffee Public-Private Task Force (CPPTF) was set up to discuss further the issues covering social, economic and environmental sustainability, and was having discussions under five technical workstreams (TWS), set up as follows:

i) TWS1 Living-Prosperous Income;

ii) TWS2 Market Transparency Lead: Committee on Sustainability Assessment;

iii) TWS3 Market Policies and Institutions + Global Funding Mechanism;

iv) TWS4 Resilient Coffee Landscapes; and

v) TWS5 Sector Coordination + Inclusion of Women and Youth.

The ICC also confirmed that the 2nd CEO and Global Leaders Forum, was to be held during the fifth World Coffee Conference in Bengaluru, India. This took place on 25-27 September 2023, and considered the outcomes of the task force. The Council committed to continue to pursue efforts in proposing concrete solutions to the coffee crisis and the price volatility issue.

The discussions of the technical workstreams were going on at the writing of this book, and ICO's vision in this is for "a sustainable and prosperous future for coffee producers and the sector as a whole."

The Third WCPF Global Meeting

Due to COVID-19 disruptions, the third forum convened after four and a half years—held in Kigali, Rwanda, on the 13th and 14th of February 2023. The pervasive poverty among coffee producers and the need for a roadmap in addressing the concerns was high on the agenda. Jamie Coats' presentation on the multidimensional poverty index sparked much debate and discussion. Noting that discussions at the various meetings had repeatedly decried the plight of coffee farmers, arguing that the producers need to have a 'living income,' the Forum postulated that farmers required prosperous income, not just survival.

At the Kigali meeting, some questions asked of the participants brought out some interesting responses, one of which was, 'is the pursuit of living income enough or should we see it as a step towards prosperity?' In one of the groups, the response was that farmers are yet to attain a living income — that living income is necessary but insufficient and only an essential measure on the way to desired prosperity. The farmers acknowledged that the pursuit of living income was appreciated. However, it needed to be seen as the initial step towards prosperity and not necessarily sufficient on its own. The farmers said that prosperity does not necessarily mean having a lot of money; you have to make smart investments to keep it. Living income may lead to living a better life and in a sustainable way — and if you get it, invest it, monitor it and keep it sustainably.

The Living Income Debate

Participants in the 2023 World Coffee Producers Forum reiterated that although the idea of living income had been presented as a solution, more was needed, and knowledge was necessary to support the income. They argued that for the living income approach to be sustainable there needed to be a balance between income and expenses. Coffee farmers reiterated that their earnings needed to lead to household prosperity. However, most acknowledged the need for financial literacy to manage their finances well, including a smart and prudent investment plan for the income earned. To achieve prosperity, the farmers also acknowledged the need for income diversification to reduce the dependency on a singular source of income and livelihood. They also indicated the need for skills, investment knowledge, and an essential grasp of the laws and regulations to ensure legal compliance.

Participants noted that much talk had ensued regarding living incomes for farmers but that the levels had not yet been determined for most sectors. Moreover, there needed to be more consideration of all the farmers' needs and what was necessary for them to live a life of dignity. Some of the issues noted were: (a) the cost of production, which is usually higher than the income received by farmers for the crop and other incomes combined; (b) generally low yields as compared to the basis on which the incomes are expected; (c) expensive farm inputs and farming activities; and (d) low prices for the farm products that are insufficient for supporting a living income.

The farmers argued that their living expenses, including food, health, education and other household requirements, were much higher than the incomes received, with many farmers subsidised by family members working in the cities. They decried the lack of direct linkages between producers and consumers, noting that the multiplicity of intermediaries in-between reduces their income, and argued that the discussion of living income must be seen as the first step towards prosperity, thus as the foundation stone to build on in ensuring prosperous income levels.

Achieving prosperity will demand continuous hard work by household members, except children for whom going to school is a must, though they participate in family chores after school. While much is said about undesirable child labour, the farmers generally said that in most cases, the children support their parents in the work that sustains the family. Indeed, the children's contribution to family labour is part of their responsible adulthood training. Child labour would amount to children engaged as full-time workers or employees in plantations and factories where they do not go to school and have no rights as children!

Concern was expressed about climate change and its impact on the future of coffee and the producers, noting that there were many new pests and diseases due to higher temperatures in coffee-growing areas, significantly affecting the yields and increasing the cost of production.

National Coffee Sustainability Plans

The WCPF took note of the recommendation from Prof Sachs' report that outlined the need for national coffee sustainability plans as critical and urgent. The approach and strategies in working towards producers' sustainability would vary from country to country. Still, a general framework is required to consider all critical issues. A template would be provided for each country to prepare its plan and strategies. The multidimensional poverty index was to be a critical part of the metrics in assessing how poverty profiles were being addressed and the sensitisation of producers in the achievement of the SDGs.

Resolutions and Declaration from the Third WCPF Global Meeting

From the discussions held in the different breakout groups, major issues were filtered and crafted into resolutions and the Kigali Declaration of 2023. The roles of the different parties were highlighted, and collaborative efforts were encouraged in order to achieve the desired sustainability of global coffee production. Below is the declaration.

Third World Coffee Producers Forum

Kigali Declaration

The third edition of the World Coffee Producers Forum was held in the city of Kigali, Rwanda, on February 13 and 14, 2023.

Considering

1. That the first Forum that was held in Colombia in 2017 raised worldwide awareness to the need for economic sustainability in global coffee supply. However, there has not been effective engagement from the other sectors in the coffee value chain to improve coffee producers' remuneration.

2. That the second Forum that was held in Brazil in 2019 highlighted the need for interaction among all agents in the value chain for the development of global actions in addition to those already carried out in each country, with co-responsibility of all public and private agents in the coffee trade to guarantee the implementation of sustainability in its economic, environmental and social dimensions.

3. That such interactions should include all the links in the value chain in a systematic manner including all stakeholders in Producing Countries.

4. That designing and implementing National Coffee Sustainability Plans is necessary to achieve prosperity for coffee producers.

5. That the meeting in Kigali was hosted by the Government of Rwanda through the National Agricultural Export Development Board, and officially opened by Hon. Dr. Gerardine Mukeshimana, Minister of Agriculture and Animal Resources.

6. That the opening ceremony had high level speakers including HE Hailemariam Desalegn, Former Prime Minister of Ethiopia, Prof. Jeffrey Sachs, Dr. Jamie Coats, Dr. Vanusia Nogueira, Amb. Solomon Rutega, Mr. Claude Bizimana, CEO of the National Agricultural Export Development Board and Dr. Juan Esteban Orduz, Chairman of the Forum.

7. That the meeting in Kigali gathered 1,020 attendees from 43 Countries who discussed the most relevant topics for coffee producers and came to the following conclusions and made the following recommendations:

Does living income lead to prosperity?

Deliberations and Conclusions

- Living Income means survival income and it is not enough.

- The cost of production is not always covered and paying

farmers below the cost of production is an injustice.

• The cost of production is increasing due to price of inputs and additional requirements of industry like certification, transition to regenerative agriculture etc.

• Farmers should be compensated by good prices and also for their efforts to increase productivity leading to the improvement on income generation, thus contributing to prosperity.

• Living Income alone does not allow farmers to have disposable income and savings, the ability to invest, deal with crisis such as COVID-19, and environmental stresses and pressure.

Recommendations

• The coffee value chain should pursue the prosperity and sustainability of coffee farmers.

• The coffee value chain should change its mindset from Living Income as a final goal and make Prosperity and Sustainability the final goal.

Is climate change the end of coffee?

Deliberations and Conclusions

• Climate change is happening already: it is affecting the livelihoods of coffee farmers who are becoming even more vulnerable and impacting the quality and quantity of coffee produced.

Recommendations

• There is a continuous need for:

o Knowledge transfer and capacity building on Good Agricultural Practices including diversification, regenerative agriculture and agroforestry to farmers.

o Research on climate resilient varieties.

o Alternative strategies in integrated farm management.

• The world needs to value the service of coffee to the environment by rewarding the farmers for their current positive contribution. The current models of Payment for Environmental Services and/or carbon credits should consider the reality of the coffee landscapes.

• Additional private and public impact investment is critical and should be collaborative.

• The role and voice of the youth and women are key.

Will increased environmental regulations in consuming countries save the planet or ruin farmers?

Deliberations and Conclusions

• The climate crisis has been primarily caused by Developed Countries and not Developing Countries.

• Environmental legislations are important but in order for

their effective implementation they should be inclusive of the entire coffee value chain. As the laws stand now and those being proposed, they are consumer-driven and non-inclusive of the coffee farmer who is the basic link of the coffee value chain, and instrumental for the protection of the environment.

- International environmental and agricultural related regulations in Consuming Countries can be well intentioned, but can have very negative impact on farmers unless they are informed and engaged.

Recommendations

- Legislators and regulators should educate themselves well and visit Producing Countries to understand the reality on the ground.

- Clear information regarding the laws should be provided.

- Consider coffee trees cultivation as afforestation and carbon credit inclusive.

- Avail support through funding and other compensating mechanisms to achieve the expected practical results from the regulations/laws.

- Adequate transition time should be given for the implementation of the laws and regulations.

- The cost of implementation of regulations imposed by Consuming Countries should be borne by such Countries.

Mandate

Considering the above-highlighted points, the attendees at this meeting request the World Coffee Producers Forum to continue the work proposed to deliver the guidelines for Producing Countries to develop "SDG-based National Coffee Sustainability Plans to Achieve Farmers' Prosperity" together with relevant stakeholders and partners.

Conclusion

The WCPF offers a platform for coffee producers to engage, collaborate, learn, and advocate for their interests while addressing the challenges and opportunities in the global industry. The WCPF encourages research and development initiatives focused on coffee production and sustainability. This includes promoting scientific studies, innovation, and technology transfer to address challenges such as climate change, pests, diseases, and quality improvement. The WCPF is advocating the engagement of different partners to support producing countries to develop their national sustainable coffee strategies that would consider all the identified concerns and work towards eliminating poverty in farming communities. The next chapter discusses various innovations that are intended to improve producers' earnings.

ABOVE: *Barista training has been growing in the producing countries, contributing to improved domestic consumption. (Photo courtesy of UCDA)*

BELOW: *A French press is used by some who like full-bodied and flavourful coffee. It is a manual coffee maker with a cylindrical carafe as a plunger with a built-in filter that percolates the coffee. The French press uses freshly boiled water to steep coarse grinds for about four minutes. (Photo courtesy of ORGANOKAWA)*

ABOVE: *Improvement in coffee quality and packaging in producing countries, like Uganda, offers several options for consumers. (Photo courtesy of ORGANOKAWA)*

BELOW: *There is a greater selection of coffee options in many producing countries, like Tanzania, including locally produced and imported brands, giving consumers opportunity to taste local offerings. (Photo courtesy of David Sseppuuya)*

ABOVE: *Prof Jeffrey Sachs (centre) chatting with Madhu Bopanna, a delegate from India, during the Second World Coffee Producers Forum conference in Campinas, Brazil, in July 2019. The renown economist was the keynote speaker. (Photo courtesy of WCPF)*

BELOW: *A cross-section of delegates at the Second World Coffee Producers Forum conference*

ABOVE: *A café at the Mount Meru Hotel in Arusha, Tanzania, offers an outlet for farmers' coffee and provides employment. Such enterprises are growing in many producing countries and provide hope for addressing poverty by guaranteeing domestic markets for farmers' coffee. (Photo courtesy of David Sseppuuya)*

BELOW, LEFT: *The writer, Fred Kawuma, with Colombian Juan Valdez in Colombia in July 2017. (Fred Kawuma photos).* BELOW, RIGHT: *The decor and ambience in the cafes at Mount Meru Hotel is tasteful and attractive. (Photo courtesy of David Sseppuuya)*

8

Innovations that Could Increase Producers' Earnings

Since its inception, the World Coffee Producers' Forum has discussed the promotion of coffee roasted at the origin, with various experiences shared by different producer groups. While some political leaders have mooted the idea of adding value to coffee in the producing countries and exporting a finished product, it has remained thus — a moot point. There are several complexities in presenting processed food products in consumer markets, with many hurdles. While opportunities exist for tapping into some markets, it is unrealistic to expect the export of all coffee to be a finished product. Thankfully, some initiatives have shown the viability of coffee roasted at origin, albeit not for all coffees, and are worth exploring. One of the initiatives is the farmer-ownership model, which in Uganda was piloted by NUCAFE. It is similar to an older system that was used by the Bugisu Cooperative Union before 1969 when it was scuttled by 'The Move to The Left', a socialist policy initiative that put all agricultural marketing under state control during the government referred to as 'Obote 1'.

The Farmer-Ownership Model

In Uganda, over the two decades to 2023, the National Union of Coffee Agribusiness Farmer Enterprises (NUCAFE) piloted a farmer-ownership model that brought hope to producers. The model in product marketing refers to a business model in which farmers or agricultural producers have direct ownership or significant control over marketing and distribution. It empowers farmers by allowing them to bypass middlemen or intermediaries and directly connect with consumers or end-users. NUCAFE is an organisation of coffee farmers that was created to process and sell the farmers' coffee collectively. There are several cooperatives that have now adopted this model.

By pooling their resources and leveraging their collective bargaining power, some Ugandan farmers (including the Uganda Coffee Farmers Alliance, Ankole Coffee Producers Union, Bugisu Cooperative Union, Okoro Coffee Cooperative Union, Rubanga Cooperative Society, Kibinge Cooperative Society, and others) can negotiate better prices, access larger markets, and reduce their reliance on intermediaries. The model promotes fair trade practices as it strives for farmers to receive a significant share of profits.

The AVPA Initiative

The Agency for the Valorization of Agricultural Products (AVPA), based in France, promotes coffee roasted in different origins. It is a non-profit entity that holds contests for coffee producers. The "Coffees Roasted at Origin" contests, held in Paris annually, are open to producers worldwide, with a jury of coffee professionals, culinary professionals and consumers with the palate. The contests are opportunities for producers to showcase their products and gain recognition for their efforts in the production, processing and preparation for the market.

There is a trend of green coffee being consumed by roasting onsite in producer nations. There is also an increasing willingness in consumer countries to pay more for coffees that have unique stories. Given these developments, AVPA has provided opportunities for producers — whether as individuals or producer groups such as associations or cooperatives — to partner with consumers in target markets. The producers take responsibility for roasting in the origin countries to the market specifications and requirements of the consumers and also guarantee the traceability of their coffees, as one of the conditions of participating in the contest. Producers measure themselves against the best! Exceptional entries that win medals and get international recognition on an excellent communication platform with various partners like customers and financiers.

The contest is open to all types of coffees — Arabicas, Robustas, washed, natural, plain, honey-processed, and others. Moreover, AVPA has created new categorisations that correspond to the offer of roasted coffees in the countries of origin, which allows the buyers to specify their choices, deviating from the traditional classifications defined earlier by the conventional market. In the 2023 contest, close to 200 exceptional coffees, from 25 countries on four continents, were showcased. The tasting was in two distinct parts — espresso mode or unfiltered infusion. Outstanding entries were judged to be from Brazil, Cameroon, Colombia, Cote d'Ivoire, Ecuador, Ethiopia, Gabon, Haiti, Honduras, Indonesia, Kenya, Laos, Mexico, Panama, Papua New Guinea, Peru, Philippines, Uganda, the USA (Hawaii), and Venezuela. Many other producer countries did not submit entries, but given the publicity and the resulting market opportunities, the absentees from the 2023 contest will take a keener interest. AVPA recognises that coffees will be different, taste different and have uniquenesses that need recognition, and seeks to award differentiated coffees that mitigates the historical limitations of commodities-driven value assessment. These coffees are presented to consumers as unique in the gourmet or specialty market segments.

The Taste of Harvest

Since February 2004, the annual African Fine Coffees Conference and Exhibition, hosted by the African Fine Coffees Association (AFCA), has allowed African producers to showcase their wares to international buyers, leading to business opportunities. A cupping competition of exceptional coffees, presented in a Taste of Harvest, showcases the unique coffees of Africa. Sometimes, these coffees are sold at an auction, but other times, several buyers contact the producers to make special offers. Generally, the producers are well rewarded, though not all coffees qualify as exceptional, thus leaving the bulk in the classification of commercial coffees. There are also different models of cupping competitions in producing and consuming countries aimed at identifying exceptional coffees for consumer marketing, promising higher returns. With every successful and sustainable partnership between producers and consumers, poverty among producers diminishes.

Many African countries have been building the capacity of coffee cuppers and baristas to identify exceptional samples that win medals in national cupping events, some of which proceed to the regional level. The baristas have helped improve the quality in local hotels, cafes and restaurants, creating opportunities for increased domestic consumption. Local roasteries in the producing countries avail several local coffee brands in various outlets — stores, cafes, supermarkets — creating opportunities for tourists and other visitors to buy and take back African coffee to their countries, which has created new market prospects for African producers. AFCA hosts an annual barista championship for African countries. The winner then represents the continent in the world barista championships, hence promoting Africa.

Conservation of Endangered Species

In April and May 2023, the award-winning conservationist Dr Gladys Kalema-Zikusoka, launched her book, *Walking with Gorillas*, in which she narrates her efforts to protect and conserve the endangered mountain gorillas that currently only exist in Eastern Africa. Dr Kalema-Zikusoka, who with her husband founded Conservation Through Public Health (CTPH), developed a model involving coffee and community partnerships in gorilla conservation. CTPH buys and markets the coffee grown by communities around the national park, where some of the proceeds go into gorilla conservation. The cause-related marketing presents the unique brand of 'Gorilla Conservation Coffee' sold worldwide at a premium. In a win-win relationship, the farmers, in partnership with CTPH, receive various services and obtain very good prices for their produce. The community members receive health care at the CTPH clinic; some work as tour guides in gorilla tracking. The infrastructure has dramatically improved, and CTPH has also helped develop other partnerships to improve education services for the community. The community's coffee farmers are not just in survival mode but on the way to prosperity. The CTPH model is an example of an innovative approach that involves the conservation of endangered species but could be adapted to any other cause and has the potential to provide value in all dimensions — social, economic and environmental. Kudos to the CTPH team!

Coffee Tourism

In the 1990s, there was a peak in visitors to Kenya as part of the Kenya Coffee Safari. During the 1980s and 1990s, the Kenyan government, through the Coffee Board of Kenya, embarked on a very aggressive programme of attracting international coffee enthusiasts to visit the country on an itinerary that included farm visits, national park excursions and tours of coffee establishments, including the weekly coffee auction. The same has happened in Rwanda and Ethiopia to some extent but has not been a deliberate strategy of other African countries. Coffee excursions are also arranged by some Latin American countries where they attract significant visitors from their North American neighbours. Coffee tourism possesses great potential in encouraging the appreciation of the diverse coffee cultures while also providing opportunities for extra income for producers and in the promotion of coffee to new customers.

Coffee tourism offers opportunities for both the local economies and tourists interested in coffee culture. Cuntries are able to leverage their rich heritage to attract visitors and create sustainable income streams. The opportunities include the options below.

Coffee Farm Tours

Visitors can tour coffee farms to learn about the production process, from planting and harvesting to processing and roasting. Interactive experiences, such as picking cherries or helping with processing, can engage tourists and provide a deeper understanding of production.

Coffee Tasting and Cupping

Coffee tourists can participate in tastings and cupping sessions to explore the diverse flavours and aromas. Coffee shops and roasteries can offer guided tastings and educational sessions to enhance appreciation. For example, an entrepreneur, a trader in Dubai, began to invite tourists and visitors to coffee tasting events, which evolved into a string of cafés with direct sourcing from producers in various countries. The initiative has enhanced a relationship between tourists and coffee farmers whose story is told in the cafés. The entrepreneur pays high premiums to the farmers who in turn produce high quality coffee. The entrepreneur makes personal visits to farmers in the producer countries, and refuses to deal with middlemen or third parties.

Coffee Workshops and Barista Training

Producer countries can offer workshops and training programmes on brewing techniques, latte art, and barista skills to tourists and aspiring coffee professionals. This is already happening in Latin America and the Eastern Africa region. Such workshops can generate revenue and help improve the local culture.

Coffee Museums and Exhibitions

Establishing museums or exhibitions can provide historical context and showcase the evolution of coffee production. In the case of Ethiopia and Uganda, where the origin of Arabica and Robusta, respectively, is attributed, there are opportunities to set up museums that tell the respective stories. Leveraging technology to have interactive displays, artefacts, and multimedia presentations can make these attractions engaging for visitors.

Coffee Cultural Events

Several producer countries have unique cultural festivals and they could host coffee-related festivals, competitions, and cultural events that can draw tourists and promote the local culture. Events such as barista championships, art competitions, and coffee-themed celebrations can be added to the activities that generate excitement and revenue. There are opportunities for addressing poverty among producers where proceeds can be channelled in addressing poverty among the coffee-producing communities.

Coffee Trail Tours

Developing trail routes that connect producing regions can encourage travellers to explore the coffee landscapes. This has been done in several Latin American countries and has begun to pick up in Africa. The Clarke Farm in Western Uganda, not too far from the Kibale Forest where wild Robusta coffee is in a protected area, offers tourists a unique coffee experience. Tours such as these can include visits to multiple farms, processing facilities, and scenic coffee-growing areas, which helps to promote the beverage and provides prospects for better premiums that improve farmers' earnings.

Eco-Tourism and Sustainability

Our responsibility in stewarding the environment is what can enhance the sustainability of the ecosystems that will guarantee a good future for the generations after us. Where production systems demonstrate good environmental stewardship, such promotion of sustainable and eco-friendly coffee practices can attract environmentally conscious tourists. Visitors can learn about sustainable farming techniques and witness the positive impact of responsible cultivation on local ecosystems. The Uganda Wildlife Authority developed coffee trails within the Kibale National Park for visitors to see the wild coffee and hear the story of the origin of Robusta. The farmers in the areas around the park are engaged in community conservation efforts and their coffee is sold at a premium for their eco-friendly practices.

Culinary Experiences

Coffee tourism can extend to culinary experiences that incorporate coffee into local cuisine. Cafés and restaurants can offer coffee-infused dishes and beverages, creating a unique culinary experience. Each producer country has a unique culinary culture which, if blended with their coffee products and offerings, could be another attraction. However, given the health aspects, it would be imperative that local medical authorities certify the offerings to ensure compliance with health standards and give assurance to visitors.

Souvenirs and Local Products

In many coffee-producing countries, there are displays of local art in various forms. In coffee tourism, local artisans can create related souvenirs and products, such as coffee-themed art, crafts, and coffee beans for purchase. Such products can be mementoes for tourists and support local businesses.

Accommodation and Lodging

Coffee-themed accommodations, such as farm stays or boutique coffee-themed hotels, can cater to enthusiasts. These lodgings can provide a unique and immersive experience.

To give visitors a good experience, there are certain investments that will need to be made by the local authorities or governments. It is imperative that producing countries invest in infrastructure, marketing, and training. Moreover, sustainable and ethical practices in coffee production can further enhance the appeal of coffee tourism destinations. The national tourism promotion agencies need to seriously consider how to include coffee tourism in their promotional programmes and to actively support the local industry in developing packages that would appeal to international visitors.

Coffee and Carbon Sequestration

Carbon sequestration is the capturing and storing of carbon dioxide (CO2) from the atmosphere, effectively removing it and storing it in natural or artificial reservoirs. It is an essential mechanism for mitigating climate change by reducing the concentration of greenhouse gases in the atmosphere. Plants and trees naturally absorb CO2 from the atmosphere through photosynthesis, converting it into organic carbon compounds. This process occurs in forests, grasslands, wetlands, and other natural ecosystems, and coffee trees, as part of terrestrial ecosystems, deserve consideration as useful for carbon sequestration and to receive the financial benefits. Just like other trees, coffee trees are effective at capturing and storing carbon, given that they absorb CO2 during photosynthesis and store it in their biomass. The carbon can remain stored for centuries, depending on the ecosystem and management practices. Some coffee farmers have engaged in enhanced carbon sequestration practices such as afforestation, planting trees in previously non-forested areas and sustainable land management techniques. These practices help increase the capacity of ecosystems to absorb and store carbon. Such coffee farmers deserve to be rewarded, for they are contributing to slowing down the rate of global warming and towards a more sustainable future.

Farmers need support to benefit from carbon credits, which can be sold on the carbon market, generating additional income. Carbon credits can also incentivise farmers to adopt sustainable farming practices that reduce greenhouse gas emissions. Traditionally, coffee farmers' income depends on the market price, which is generally volatile, and participation in carbon credit programmes will mitigate that.

With carbon sequestration, there is likely to be more resilience because many sustainable farming practices that qualify for carbon credits also contribute to increased productivity. For example, agroforestry systems, which involve planting trees alongside coffee crops, can provide shade, improve soil health, reduce water evaporation, and provide habitat for beneficial organisms. Most farmers are smallholders and need technical assistance to take advantage of carbon credit programmes. Such arrangements will provide access to much-needed services, including training in implementation of sustainable farming practices, and can include guidance on agroforestry techniques, soil conservation, water management, and other sustainable practices.

Coffee produced under sustainable farming practices, and is certified through carbon credit programmes, can be marketed as environmentally friendly and socially responsible. Such market differentiation can attract environmentally conscious consumers and specialty coffee buyers who are willing to pay premium prices for sustainably produced coffee. Leveraging carbon credits allows coffee farmers to differentiate their products and access higher-value markets.

It is worth noting that the specific benefits and mechanisms for coffee farmers to access carbon credits may vary depending on the carbon credit programme, certification standards, and regional contexts. Engaging with local agricultural cooperatives, NGOs, or specialised carbon credit organisations can guide farmers in navigating the carbon credit landscape. Unfortunately, a closed-loop system seems to lock farmers out of the real benefits of the global trade in carbon credits. A carbon credit that is generated in the Global North can fetch more than ten times the one that is generated in Africa.

Other Products from Coffee

Research indicates that various by-products and derivatives can be obtained from coffee beyond its traditional use as a beverage, which could add to the value that can go back to the producer. Some are given below.

Oil: Oil is extracted from coffee beans and is used in the cosmetic industry. It contains antioxidants and has moisturising properties, making it suitable for skincare products like lotions, creams, and lip balms.

Extracts: Extracts are concentrated forms of coffee flavour. They are used in the food industry to add flavour to products such as ice cream, chocolates, desserts, and baked goods.

Skincare Products: Coffee is known for its skincare benefits. Ground coffee or extracts are used in scrubs, masks, and body washes to exfoliate, brighten the skin, and reduce the appearance of cellulite.

Dyes: Coffee can be used as a natural dye for fabrics and papers. Different shades of brown are made by soaking in brewed coffee or applying coffee grounds, resulting in a unique and eco-friendly dyeing method. Special paints are weather-resistant, and if used on walls or as car paints, they will not quickly fade as many ordinary paints do.

Grounds: After brewing, the leftover grounds can be repurposed as a natural exfoliant in skin care products, added to compost for enriching soil, or utilised as a natural odour absorber like in baby diapers.

Flour: Flour can be made from the dried pulp of coffee parchment which, usually, is discarded during primary processing. The parchment husks are processed into fibre-rich flour, antioxidants, and protein. The flour can also be used in baking, and in making smoothies and other culinary applications. Coffee flour production should conform to local health standards and food safety regulations.

Liqueur: Coffee liqueur is a popular alcoholic beverage that infuses beans or extracts into spirits like vodka or rum. It is often used as an ingredient in cocktails or enjoyed independently. There are some well-known liqueurs such as Irish Coffee, Grand French Coffee, Cafe Com Cheirinho, Caffee Corretto, Kahlua and Monk's Coffee. We have already seen that coffee is rich in antioxidants and may offer modest heart health benefits. However, alcohol consumption has its challenges, and the benefits of the coffee liqueur would best be appropriated if consumed only occasionally. Several African countries and other producer regions have innovated with liqueurs.

Soap: Soap helps exfoliate the skin and help remove dead skin cells, promoting skin renewal and a youthful appearance. Coffee soap, like regular coffee or coffee extracts, may offer some anti-ageing benefits due to the presence of antioxidant compounds. When coffee is used in soap, the antioxidants, such as chlorogenic and caffeic acid, may be absorbed through the skin. Skin ageing happens due to the constant exposure of the skin to various environmental stressors that can lead to the formation of free radicals. Thus, antioxidants in coffee soap can help neutralise these free radicals, reducing oxidative stress on the skin and potentially slowing down the ageing process. By protecting the skin from damage caused by ultra violet rays, pollution, and other factors, coffee soap may also help maintain skin elasticity and reduce the appearance of fine lines and wrinkles.

Scented Candles: Coffee-scented candles create cosy and aromatic ambience. They are made by infusing coffee fragrance into candle wax, giving off a pleasant coffee aroma when burned. Moreover, as coffee farmers engage in bee-keeping, the bee hives' wax can be used to make candle wax. The candles offer various benefits beyond their pleasant aroma. Here are some potential advantages of using coffee-scented candles:

Aromatherapy: Coffee's scent has mood-enhancing properties and can create a calming and cosy ambience. For coffee lovers, the aroma can evoke positive feelings and reduce stress or anxiety.

Increased Focus and Alertness: Coffee's scent is often associated with increased focus and alertness. Inhaling the aroma through a candle might provide a subtle boost in mental alertness and concentration.

Odour Elimination: Coffee-scented candles can help mask or eliminate unwanted odours in your living space, leaving a pleasant fragrance instead.

Relaxation: The warm and inviting scent of coffee can help create a relaxing atmosphere, making scented candles ideal for unwinding after a long day or setting a soothing mood during leisure activities.

Nostalgia: For those who enjoy the smell of coffee, the scented candles can evoke feelings of nostalgia and comfort, reminding them of coffee shops or cosy mornings with a fresh brew.

Alternative to Brewing Coffee: Some people love the coffee aroma but are highly sensitive to the beverage. Even such people can enjoy the benefits of the aroma without drinking coffee! Lighting a scented candle can provide the pleasant aroma without brewing a cup, which is particularly useful if one is sensitive to caffeine or wants to enjoy the scent without drinking the beverage. The benefits of scented candles primarily come from the aromatic experience and the psychological effects of the scent rather than any direct health effects associated with coffee consumption.

Complementing Home Decor: Scented candles add a warm and inviting touch to your home decor, enhancing the overall ambience and making your living space feel more welcoming.

Innovators keep developing ideas for new uses beyond the traditional use of coffee as a beverage. All this is exciting, as every new idea comes with a new promise to the coffee producer that more uses also imply fresh hopes of better prices. The above examples are just a few of the diverse range of products that can be derived from coffee. As it continues to inspire creativity and innovation, more possibilities for utilising coffee by-products are being explored in various industries. As with any skincare product, individual results may vary, and it is essential to choose products that suit one's skin type and consider potential allergies or sensitivities. For significant anti-ageing benefits, a well-rounded skincare routine that includes sunscreen, moisturisers, and targeted anti-ageing products might be more effective when combined with a balanced diet and a healthy lifestyle.

Conclusion

The problem of poverty in coffee-producing countries is multifaceted and does not have simple, straightforward solutions. It instead requires a strategic and systems approach. Many systems need overhauling, from the producer level to the final processing and retail. Partnerships with producers must be seen as critical to the business model's success because a social entrepreneurial approach that ensures that producers are actual beneficiaries will lead to a win-win outcome. The moot point of many political leaders is that all the coffee in the producing countries can be exported as a finished product, which raises many hopes but could become very frustrating because the market dynamics are quite complicated. The complexities in presenting processed food products in consumer markets could only be handled where viable partnerships exist between producers and the final consumers. The form of partnerships will vary, but such opportunities exist and are worthy of pursuit. The next chapter discusses transformational ideas.

9

Transformational Ideas

In addressing poverty among coffee farmers, it is crucial to consider implementing a combination of transformation ideas that can disrupt the industry. The ideas must be tailored to the specific context of each producer country to contribute to a more equitable and sustainable coffee trade, ensuring that farmers receive a fair share of the value created throughout the supply chain. Producer countries facing the challenge of an imbalance in trade and the disparity between the price of coffee at the origin and the price paid by the final consumer can consider several transformation ideas. Some strategies can include value addition, direct trade and fair trade, reforming cooperatives or empowering producer organisations to participate in dismantling the poverty profile.

Direct Trade

Encouraging direct trade between coffee producers and buyers can help eliminate some unnecessary intermediaries. This would ensure that a larger portion of the revenue goes to the producers. For example, adopting Fairtrade practices can provide coffee farmers with better prices and improved living conditions.

Strengthening Producer Organisations

Strengthening and promoting the formation of cooperatives can help consolidate farmers' bargaining power. In many countries, farmers operate without association or agglomeration; where they are present, they are often weak and have poor governance structures. Strengthening cooperatives can enable farmers to collectively negotiate prices, access finance, and invest in shared processing facilities, reducing costs and increasing profitability. Strengthened producer organisations are in a better and more strategic position to apply the farmer-ownership model and reap its benefits.

Quality Improvement

Investing in techniques to enhance quality can lead to better prices. This would involve training farmers in best agricultural practices, implementing quality control measures, and establishing certification programmes such as organic and other environmentally friendly practices or specialty coffee production. Value-adding measures can significantly improve the farmers' earnings but should not be seen in isolation from the initiatives that improve market access and give better returns.

Diversification

Producer countries can explore diversification by cultivating other high-value crops, which can reduce reliance on coffee as the sole source of income and provide additional revenue streams, contributing to economic stability and resilience. One of the proposals of the World Coffee Producers' Forum is to encourage national coffee sustainability plans. The WCPF hopes that each country will adopt appropriate diversification measures.

Beekeeping

Beekeeping is a diversification activity. Owing to increased population pressure and human activity that has disrupted the natural habitats of pollinating insects, adversely affecting biodiversity, crop yields have reduced due to poor pollination. Beekeeping, in addition to having shade trees that provide bird habitats, helps address the ecological imbalance and is good for the environment. Testimonies of Ugandan coffee farmers who adopted beekeeping, as narrated to a media person working for one international development agency, indicated that they had turned from poor, miserable farmers to prosperous ones as the bees brought them a two-fold benefit.

First, they reported significant yields from the coffee trees, resulting from improved pollination, and then additional revenue from selling honey. One farmer, who cultivated 20 acres, described how they had achieved a 32 per cent increase in coffee productivity by introducing bee hives. Another reported that they had introduced bees on their 30-acre farm by putting up 100 colonised hives and other hives in shades of trees. The farmers reported increased yields, with bigger and healthier beans in all cases. This resonated with empirical studies carried out by scientists who studied the impact of beekeeping on coffee yields in different countries, where an average increase of 25 per cent was recorded. This, coupled with the income from honey, with possibilities of other farm-income streams, contributes to income diversification. Support, in terms of extension services and social entrepreneurship initiatives, could go a long way in building the capacity of the farmers and addressing the poverty.

Sustainable Practices

Adopting sustainable agricultural practices can contribute to the production of higher-quality coffee while minimising environmental impact. Certification programmes, such as UTZ Rainforest Alliance, can enhance market access and fetch premium prices for sustainably produced coffee. The sustainability approaches farmers adopt must lead to long-term improvement and prosperity.

Technology Adoption

Embracing technology and innovation in coffee production, processing, and distribution can lead to efficiency gains and cost reductions. This includes advanced farming techniques, improving post-harvest processing, and exploring e-commerce platforms for direct consumer sales. Of course, farmers need training in the adoption and use of the appropriate technology to obtain the desired benefits.

Value Addition

Producer countries can focus on adding value to their coffee by processing it into higher-value products, as discussed in Chapter Eight regarding other products. Value addition includes roasting, packaging, and local branding. Many other products can be extracted from coffee to feed into the cosmetics, healthcare, and culinary industries.

The traditional value-addition model should not be seen by producers as the magic solution or silver bullet to solve all their problems. This notwithstanding, producers could capture a larger share of the final retail price by moving up the value chain directly (with attendant challenges) or through mutually beneficial partnerships. Partnership ideas could include, but are not restricted to the following:

Direct Trade Relationships: Establishing direct trade links between producers and consumers allows for closer collaboration and transparency throughout the supply chain. By bypassing intermediaries, producers can receive a higher share of the final price, while consumers can have more visibility into the origin and quality of the coffee they purchase. This sounds easy, but in practice it has many hurdles to surmount. Appropriate strategies have to be worked out to ensure that the needs and concerns of all parties are addressed.

Specialty Coffee Programmes: Collaborating on specialty programmes can create opportunities for value addition. Producers can focus on cultivating specialty varieties, using meticulous processing techniques, and adhering to specific quality standards. This partnership enables consumers to access unique and high-quality coffee while providing a premium price to producers. A pledge from the specialty retailer that informs the consumers of a specific portion of the retail price that goes back as an extra benefit to the farmers would significantly address the farmer's poverty.

Roaster-Farmer Partnerships: Coffee roasters can form partnerships directly with farmers or cooperatives to ensure a consistent supply of quality beans. These partnerships can involve sharing knowledge and expertise on processing and roasting techniques, allowing farmers to enhance their quality and increase the value of their products. A win-win partnership will address issues of the farmers' sustainability in their ecosystems, thus ensuring a sustainable approach that meets the global development goals outlined by the United Nations.

Sustainability Initiatives: Partnering on sustainability initiatives can add value to coffee production and consumption. Producers and consumers can work together to implement environmentally friendly practices, such as promoting organic farming, supporting reforestation efforts, or investing in renewable energy solutions. This partnership can create a shared commitment to sustainability and resonate with environmentally conscious consumers.

Branding and Marketing Collaborations: Producers and consumers can collaborate on branding and marketing to promote the origin and unique qualities of the coffee. Joint marketing, storytelling, and packaging design collaborations highlighting the producers' story, heritage, and sustainable practices are recommended.

Consumer Education and Engagement: Collaboration can focus on educating consumers about the production process, including the challenges producers face and the importance of fair trade. Farm visits, interactive workshops, or online platforms that provide information about coffee's origin, cultivation, and processing can be effective platforms.

Supply Chain Traceability: Working together to establish transparent and traceable supply chains can build trust between producers and consumers. With blockchain technology or other traceability systems, consumers can have access to information about the origin, certifications, and fair-trade practices associated with the coffee they purchase, fostering a deeper connection with the producers.

Product Development: Producers and consumers can collaborate on product development to create new and innovative coffee-related products. This can include ready-to-drink coffee beverages, coffee-infused food products, or coffee-related accessories. Joint product development can cater to evolving consumer preferences and create additional revenue streams for producers.

Implementation of Partnerships

When forming partnerships around value-addition, it is critical that both producers and consumers have clear communication, trust, and a shared vision of sustainability and fairness in the industry. Partnerships around value-addition have led to mutual benefits, improved quality, increased market access, and more equitable and sustainable coffee trade. The examples below are not endorsements of the companies or organisations involved but are intended to highlight specific efforts worth scaling up. They are:

Café Direct and Smallholder Farmers: Café Direct, a UK-based company, has established long-term partnerships with smallholder farmers in various countries in Latin America and Africa. Through these partnerships, Café Direct provides technical assistance, access to finance, and training to farmers, helping them improve their coffee quality, increase yields, and implement sustainable farming practices. In return, Café Direct receives a consistent supply of high-quality coffee beans and ensures that a fair share of the revenue goes back to the farmers.

Fairtrade International and Retailers: Fairtrade International is a global organisation that promotes fair trade practices and supports small-scale farmers. Through their cooperatives, the smallholder farmers partner with retailers, such as coffee shop chains and grocery stores, to ensure that Fairtrade-certified coffee is available to consumers. This partnership helps improve farmers' livelihoods by guaranteeing fair prices and providing additional premiums for social and environmental projects. It also increases market access for small-scale producers by connecting them with consumers who prioritise ethical and sustainable products.

Nespresso AAA Sustainable Quality Program: Nespresso has partnered with the Rainforest Alliance to establish the AAA Sustainable Quality Program, which focuses on working directly with farmers to improve quality, promote sustainable practices, and ensure fair prices. Nespresso provides farmers with training, technical assistance, and financial support in exchange for access to high-quality coffee beans. The partnership benefits both parties by enhancing quality, ensuring a consistent supply for Nespresso, and supporting farming communities' economic and environmental sustainability.

Cooperative Coffees and Specialty Coffee Roasters: Cooperative Coffees is a green coffee importing cooperative based in North America. They have established partnerships with specialty roasters who share a commitment to sustainability and fair trade. Cooperative Coffees helps improve market access and prices for farmers by directly sourcing the produce from small-scale cooperatives around the world. The roasters benefit from access to high-quality, traceable coffees while ensuring that a fair share of the revenue goes back to the producer cooperatives.

Starbucks and Conservation International: Starbucks, a global coffee chain, has collaborated with Conservation International, an environmental organisation, in an initiative called the Coffee and Farmer Equity (C.A.F.E.) Practices programme. The partnership promotes sustainable farming practices, improves farmer livelihoods, and ensures high-quality produce. Starbucks provides technical assistance, access to credit, and premium prices to farmers who meet the C.A.F.E. Practices criteria. Some reports indicate that the partnership has improved coffee quality, increased incomes for farmers, and enhanced environmental stewardship in coffee-producing regions.

These examples highlight the potential of value-addition partnerships to create more equitable and sustainable trade. By fostering collaboration, transparency, and fair-trade, these partnerships have brought positive change to producers, improved product quality, and catered to consumer demand for ethically sourced and sustainable coffee.

Market Development

Producer countries can invest in marketing and promoting their coffee in key markets. Creating a distinct brand identity and engaging in targeted marketing campaigns can help increase consumer awareness and demand, enabling countries to command higher prices. Several countries, like Colombia, Ethiopia, Brazil, Rwanda, and Costa Rica have invested in marketing and promoting their coffee in key consumer markets to increase their products' awareness, demand, and value. For these countries, it has been a significant investment over a long period, not just intermittent or sporadic market interventions. The dividends become increasingly evident for each of these, and much more needs to be done. Below are highlights:

Colombia is renowned for its high-quality coffee and has invested significantly in global marketing. The National Federation of Coffee Growers of Colombia (FNC) launched the iconic "Juan Valdez" campaign in the 1960s, featuring a fictional coffee farmer as a brand ambassador. The campaign highlighted Colombian coffee's distinctiveness and promoted it as a premium product. The FNC also participates in international trade shows, conducts promotional events, and collaborates with coffee associations and retailers.

Ethiopia, the birthplace of coffee, has used various marketing initiatives. The Ethiopian Coffee Exporters Association (ECEA) and the Ethiopian Coffee and Tea Authority have focused on branding with the trademarked "Sidamo," "Yirgacheffe," and "Harrar" labels to emphasise their unique regional characteristics. They have also participated in international coffee events, organised coffee competitions, and facilitated direct trade relationships between their producers and international buyers.

Brazil, as the largest producer in the world, has invested in marketing to maintain its dominant position. The Brazilian Specialty Coffee Association (BSCA) promotes through targeted campaigns, participation in trade shows, and collaborations with importers, roasters, and retailers worldwide. Brazil also highlights sustainable production practices such as organic and Rainforest Alliance coffee certifications.

Rwanda, known for its specialty coffee, has strived to enhance its global presence through marketing initiatives. The National Agricultural Export Development Board (NAEB) of Rwanda promotes its produce by participating in international trade fairs, organising cupping sessions, and supporting producers in obtaining quality certifications. The "Rwanda Coffee" branding campaign emphasises the country's commitment to quality and sustainability, creating awareness and demand in international markets.

Costa Rica has implemented marketing strategies to showcase its high-quality coffee. The Costa Rican Coffee Institute (ICAFE) works through its "Café de Costa Rica" branding, highlighting its unique flavours and attributes. ICAFE participates in international events, facilitates coffee tours and tastings for visitors, and supports educational programmes to enhance consumer knowledge.

The **Inter-African Coffee Organisation (IACO)** embarked on a programme to promote domestic consumption of coffee in the IACO Member States as a way of stimulating the African domestic market. Focus on the promotion of youth and female coffee entrepreneurs is visible. As affluence and urbanisation increase in Africa, there are significant market prospects. Given that Brazil successfully promoted domestic consumption, leading to significant growth over two decades, the same approach can create prospects for African entrepreneurs who, in serving this market, can address poverty among producers. Promotion of domestic consumption is happening in several Latin American countries and in Asia, particularly Vietnam and Indonesia, an approach that should eventually create local markets to reduce export dependency, and hopefully increase farm-gate prices while reducing poverty among producers.

These examples demonstrate the efforts made by producers to differentiate their coffee offerings, highlight their unique qualities and engage with consumers in key markets. Kenya used to do it very well, but those efforts faded in the two decades since 2000. However, the others that have been persistent have achieved much through branding, participation in trade shows, collaborations with industry stakeholders, and promotional campaigns increasing visibility, value, and demand in the global marketplace.

Government Support

Governments can play a crucial role in supporting coffee farmers by implementing policies and programmes that promote the development of the coffee sector. This includes providing access to credit, investing in infrastructure, facilitating research and development, and ensuring a supportive regulatory environment. The role of governments is indisputable, although corruption or bad governance, in many cases, poses a formidable challenge.

The Need for Policy Advocacy

Coffee-producing countries can advocate international policy to address trade imbalances and promote fairer trade practices. Collaborating with other producers and participating in discussions at forums like the Inter-African Coffee Organisation (IACO), the World Coffee Producers Forum, and the International Coffee Organization (ICO) can help raise awareness and drive policy changes. The ICO must play a more proactive role in globally representing the interests of producers for the achievement of the United Nations' development goals that address poverty, economic imbalances, gender and youth empowerment and social, economic and environmental sustainability critical to producers' prosperity.

Brazilian Innovation on Instant Coffee

The Brazilian Instant Coffee Industry Association (ABICS) recently presented a white paper highlighting its research in developing a new sensory analysis protocol for instant coffee. This innovation promises to evolve into a tool that will accelerate the consumption of instant coffee. For long, there was a misconception that instant coffee is low-quality. Many people were discouraged from its consumption. The truth is that the quality of instant coffee, also known as soluble coffee, can be categorised along a continuum — from poor quality to exceptional coffee. It is a misconception that ABICS set out to address. Technological developments have greatly enhanced and improved quality of manufacturing, and the consumer has some decent choices to consider.

Redefining Instant Coffee

According to ABICS, instant coffee should not be seen as a

singular product of low quality but a complex category of varied qualities, profiles, and applications to suit the taste preferences of different consumers and markets. Given that Brazil is the world's leading coffee producer, the second largest consumer, and the global leader in the production and export of soluble coffee, it was in ABICS's interest to spearhead the search for a solution. Instant coffee is not a uniform product but one with possible classification depending on the quality of green coffee used in its production and the manufacturing process, among other factors. Variations in the manufacturing processes include whether the produce was sprayed or freeze-dried, as well as the pressure of extraction and varying combinations of temperatures in the extraction process.

Development of a Quality Protocol for Instant Coffee

Thus, ABICS, in partnership with the ITAL Food Tech Institute, a governmental body and a reference in research and development and technological innovation in Latin America, developed a ground-breaking methodology for identifying flavour attributes specific to instant coffee. The protocol involved a thorough analysis of the various factors, aiming to achieve a common quality assessment and grading system. It is hoped that when the communication to consumers highlights the truth about soluble coffee, its differentiation and its unique attributes, there is potential to reinvigorate the desire to enjoy a cup of coffee with greater ease and convenience. According to ABICS, diversity and differentiation in the soluble coffee category have existed, but an effective communication strategy to customers has been lacking.

The team developed a sensory lexicon which they specifically refined for instant coffee and then used it to differentiate instant coffee's key attributes. A sensory lexicon is a tool used to describe and quantify sensory attributes of food, beverages, and personal care products. In the above case, the ABICS team developed one specifically for instant coffee to meet consumer expectations and preferences. This lexicon's attributes are similar to those of roasted and ground coffee lexicons, such as sweetness, acidity, and body. The attributes exclusive to the instant coffee category included 'over-extracted coffee flavour'. Adopting a five-point intensity scale to describe the attributes would have been simplistic. However, preference was given to descriptions of three grades of instant coffee: *excellent instant coffee*; *differentiated instant coffee;* and *conventional instant coffee*. The team agreed that one coffee was not actually better than the other, but attributes of certain coffees made them particularly suitable for specific applications. For instance, the instant coffee used in the now popular three-in-one would be different from what is sold as the Nescafe Gold blend.

Lessons and Precedents from the Specialty Coffee Association

When the specialty movement began in the United States in the 1990s, the Specialty Coffee Association (SCA) developed a sensory evaluation protocol to grade what qualified specialty coffee. By setting up the Coffee Quality Institute (CQI), the SCA and its partners developed a protocol and set up a system to train quality analysts and coffee cuppers who followed the protocol. The SCA and CQI instituted a new protocol which ABICS now advocates for instant coffee. Adopting a standard system in assessing the quality of instant coffee, grading, and effective communication to consumers has excellent potential to open the door to the diverse and differentiated coffee options in the instant category. The standardised protocol allows for continuous quality improvement, and provide countless possibilities of combinations of the raw material and production process in creating and discovering new combinations and beverages. This transformational development will help strategically position soluble coffees to a new global standard!

ABICS trains industry professionals as instant coffee (IC) graders who, after their calibration, will become certified as IC Graders. Afterwards, training for baristas and other coffee professionals will follow. ABICS was also planning to develop a quality seal first for the domestic Brazilian market and then for export markets, intended to revolutionise the soluble coffees market. The Brazilian innovation was aiming to present a clear identification to consumers to appreciate the category and attributes of the instant products so that they can make informed decisions in line with their tastes and preferences. There are various blends and qualities of instant coffee worldwide, with different packaging and various preparations. The numerous uses of soluble coffee as reflected in versatility and growth in consumption in different markets is an excellent opportunity to meet consumer demands and requirements.

The Global Coffee Platform

The Global Coffee Platform (GCP), with its headquarters in Bonn, Germany, is a sustainability-focused organisation that brings together a wide range of stakeholders. It developed the 'Coffee Sustainability Reference Code' to provide a common language for baseline sustainability, as well as an equivalence mechanism that guides users of different systems to identify how they relate to the above code. GCP advocates continuous improvement which is also evidenced in what started as the Common Code for the Coffee Community (4C) in 2004, when the 4C Code was launched, evolving into the 4C Association in 2007, as a multi-stakeholder membership platform. In 2016, the 4C Association further evolved into the GCP. In that year the premier version of the GCP Equivalence Mechanism was published, and the code itself was, in 2021, renamed the Coffee Sustainability Code.

The GCP has set for itself the goal of achieving transformational change in farmer prosperity for more than one million farmers in ten countries by 2030.

The GCP aims to address the sustainability challenges faced by the global coffee industry by promoting collaboration, knowledge sharing, and collective action. The GCP acts as a neutral platform facilitating dialogue and partnership among stakeholders, including coffee producers, traders, roasters, retailers, civil society organisations, and governments. It promotes sustainable production and consumption by supporting and implementing best practices related to environmental, social, and economic aspects of production, which involves addressing climate change, deforestation, water management, labour rights, and market access. The GCP encourages collaboration and alignment among stakeholders to create a unified approach. By working together, the platform seeks to enhance the effectiveness of sustainability initiatives and avoid duplication. The GCP recognises that supply chains are very complex, but the platform works to see how to reduce the living income gap.

Conclusion

Many transformational ideas are springing up all over the world, and they need to be harnessed to ensure the industry's sustainability by giving better returns to producers. The tailoring of ideas to the specific context of each coffee-producing country will contribute to the sustainable and desired future for the global value chain, where the producers are key nodes. It is also critical to consider and resolve the logistical nightmares involved in the delivery of coffee from the origin to the target consumers – a matter that has several complexities that must be addressed for competitiveness, without which no business or initiative can survive. Coffee-producing countries facing the challenge of trade imbalance and undesirable poverty among the farming communities need to benefit from the numerous transformation ideas cropping up. The next chapter outlines the pathway to prosperity for coffee producers.

10

The Path to Prosperity for Coffee Producers

For coffee producers to prosper, all the different players in the value chain would need to play their roles. There has to be a pathway to achieve this prosperity, which must inevitably begin with the farmers. Quality is one of the critical issues. Giving serious attention to the sustainability of the production ecosystems is also imperative. The critical components of the path should include quality improvement, adoption of sustainable practices, improved access to affordable finance, market diversification, value addition, access to knowledge and technology, strengthening cooperatives, gender inclusion and empowerment, collaboration and knowledge exchange, and policy support. Entrepreneurial skills in the producing countries are critical. However, the farmer-ownership model is perhaps one of the most effective approaches in guaranteeing prosperity for producers, as discussed in Chapter Eight, but it should be used in combination with other strategies as discussed below.

Quality Improvement

Investing in training and resources to improve coffee quality would include educating farmers on best agricultural practices, post-harvest processing techniques, and cupping skills. Higher-quality coffee can command premium prices and open doors to specialty markets.

Access to Finance

The cost of finance in most producer countries is prohibitively high, yet providing coffee producers with access to affordable credit and financial services can help them make farm investments. Such help could support upgrading equipment, improving infrastructure, or expanding production. Financial inclusion empowers producers to navigate market fluctuations and invest in growing their businesses.

Market Diversification

Encouraging producers to diversify their market access can involve exploring specialty coffee markets, direct trade relationships, and niche consumer segments. By diversifying their customer base, producers can reduce their dependence on volatile commodity markets and capture higher-value opportunities. Diversified production systems that reduce dependence on coffee alone include high-value crops and aviculture, and can improve farmers' earnings if market access for those other products is also addressed.

Value Addition

Supporting coffee producers in adding value to their products can increase profitability. The value addition includes investing in processing infrastructure, promoting roasting and packaging capabilities, and fostering partnerships with local and international buyers to move up the value chain. Given the increasing potential for domestic consumption in producer countries, the value proposition for farmers investing in value addition includes increased profitability, market differentiation, expanded market access, brand building, direct consumer relationships, risk mitigation, and contributions to sustainable agriculture and rural development. These benefits can give farmers more control over their products, higher revenues, and resilience.

Access to Knowledge and Technology

Facilitating access to relevant information, training, and technology is crucial for producers. This support involves disseminating research findings, promoting innovation in farming practices, and leveraging digital tools and platforms for market intelligence, supply chain management, and marketing. Access to knowledge and technology can enhance the competitiveness and efficiency of the farmers.

Strengthening Cooperatives

Encouraging the formation and strengthening of farmer cooperatives can enhance producers' bargaining power, facilitate collective marketing, and provide economies of scale for inputs and services. Cooperatives empower farmers to negotiate better prices, access resources, and strengthen their position in the value chain. The farmer-ownership model is only possible with strong farmer organisations, including solid governance structures and financial literacy.

Youth and Gender Inclusion and Empowerment

Engaging the younger generation in the coffee value chain is critical in ensuring the long-term sustainability of the industry. In the same vein, gender equality and women's empowerment within the coffee sector is essential for sustainable development. Providing training, financial support, and leadership opportunities for the youth and women in coffee-producing communities can drive economic growth and foster more equitable outcomes.

Policy Support

Governments and industry stakeholders should create an enabling policy environment that supports producers. This includes implementing supportive trade policies, investing in rural infrastructure, facilitating access to land, providing technical assistance, and fostering collaboration among relevant actors. Good policies will enhance the agenda of creating a sustainable coffee industry while bad policies will further entrench poverty among farming communities.

Collaboration and Knowledge Exchange

Encouraging collaboration among coffee-producing countries, industry organisations, research institutions, and development agencies is vital for sharing knowledge, best practices, and resources. International platforms and initiatives can facilitate dialogue, cooperation, and collective efforts to address common challenges and identify opportunities. Knowledge is power and ignorance is a curse, which is why it is critical to promote knowledge-sharing aimed at the transformation of farming communities.

Sustainable Practices

Researchers have shown that tropical agroforestry systems, including where coffee is grown under canopies of shade trees, are a solution in conserving biodiversity as an approach that complements strict forest protection. Where biodiversity conservation contributes to benefits for the farmer, this approach would undoubtedly enhance the coffee farmers' livelihoods. In a study supported by the Swedish Research Council, conducted in 2021 in Ethiopia's forested area of Gimma, by collaborating scientists from Stockholm University and Addis Ababa University, it was noted that there were some significant coffee yield trade-offs versus different models of biodiversity.

Promoting sustainable farming practices is essential for long-term prosperity. Encouraging organic farming, agroforestry, soil conservation, and water management helps preserve the environment, maintain soil fertility, and mitigate the impact of climate change. However, it is critical to provide support to the farmers who engage in these practices and ensure that they receive the incentives to continue in these investments. This is where partnerships in the market are critical.

Conclusion

A comprehensive Path to Prosperity for coffee producers requires a holistic approach encompassing the above-mentioned dimensions. By focusing on quality, sustainability, market diversification, empowerment, and supportive policies, coffee producers can enhance their resilience, profitability, and overall well-being in the global industry. Promoting sustainable farming practices is critical for long-term prosperity. However, it has to be backed up by the necessary strategies for providing sustainable income to the producers for them to continue in the good practices. To implement the proposed strategies, there is need for the development of entrepreneurial skills among producers to engage in farming as a business. Entrepreneurial leadership in the value chain within producer countries could significantly contribute to the transformation of practices that currently perpetuate the vicious circle of poverty. The next chapter looks at the emerging issues at the global level with significant potential impact on coffee producers and their economic sustainability.

11

Conclusion and Emerging Issues

Coffee consumption has been more or less steady in most markets with modest overall growth. Scientific studies have identified health benefits associated with coffee consumption, guidelines for consumption, and caution on how to consume coffee. The challenge for producers, however, has remained the issue of low farmer earnings. The period after the COVID-19 pandemic of 2020-21 saw an improvement in prices at the commodity exchanges, though it was not sustained. Coffee that is traded on the commodity exchange will always have 'boom and bust' cycles and significantly low prices have considerable effects on producer earnings, engendering outcries about poverty entrenchment among coffee farmers worldwide. With the exception of Brazil and Vietnam, most producing countries generally have low productivity and high production costs. Different countries have developed coping mechanisms, but poverty endures among coffee-producing communities in all regions. The Oxford University model of the multidimensional poverty index shows the poverty profiles in different countries.

Several collective actions have attempted to address producer concerns through engagements that build on synergies on the consumption side of the value chain. Some initiatives are by individual entities. However, there are some emerging issues that need close examination to see whether coffee producers will be extricated from the poverty profiles that keep them in a state of slavery. One African leader stated some day in the 2020s that some players were slave masters while others served as their agents, and then asked who would help to free the slaves. This was a very strong statement!

Existing and Upcoming Legislation and Potential Impact

Europe, North America and Japan all have specific requirements for coffee to access those markets, and there are both tariff and non-tariff barriers on imports. An exporter has to meet certain legal and non-legal requirements to bring coffee in each of these jurisdictions, mostly in connection with food safety, traceability and environmental concerns. However, there are increasingly additional requirements that European buyers must comply with to target specific segments or to keep up with European market developments. At the time of writing (in 2023), there was the challenge of a lot of 'unknowns' or even estimating the cost of implementation of the EU legislation on the part of the exporters from the coffee-producing countries.

Some of the coffee trading companies in Europe are worried about the new EU legislation that could significantly increase their operational costs and potentially put some of them out of business. The concern among producers, on the other hand, is that new EU regulations will increase costs for the operators and reduce farmers' earnings. There are fears that growers will ultimately bear the bulk of the costs of compliance and will be worse off, with a significant diminishing of their income. Given that market forces — supply and demand — determine coffee prices, some producers may get better returns as a result of shrinking supply after some farmers quit coffee altogether, but those who quit could end up in worse poverty traps and reduce standards of livingamong some vulnerable rural communities in coffee-growing areas.

International Coffee Organization Initiatives

The International Coffee Organization (ICO) is an intergovernmental organisation that serves as the global commodity body specifically for coffee, under the governance of the International Coffee Council (ICC). The ICO brings together governments of coffee-producing and consuming countries and, in the agreement of 2022 that was still under ratification, made room for private sector participation in its governing structure, though without voting powers. The ICO has several initiatives to address the sustainability of smallholder coffee farmers globally, including development projects, technical assistance and capacity building, market information and promotion, and partnerships and collaborations, as described below:

1. Coffee Development Projects: The ICO implements various projects in coffee-producing countries to support smallholder farmers. They focus on improving farming practices, enhancing productivity, promoting climate resilience, fostering economic sustainability, and creating greater impact.

2. Technical Assistance and Capacity Building: The ICO provides technical assistance and capacity-building programmes to coffee-producing countries, focussing on growing the knowledge and skills of smallholder farmers in areas such as sustainable farming practices, post-harvest processing, quality control, and marketing. Due to limited resources, the ICO can provide only so much support and, let alone, bear the needs of partnerships of other agencies to address all the areas as identified or requested.

3. Market Information and Promotion: The ICO collects and disseminates market information to coffee-producing countries, including smallholder farmers, for informed decision-making. This includes data on prices, market trends, and demand. The ICO also undertakes promotional activities to raise awareness about sustainable coffee production and consumption.

4. Partnerships and Collaborations: The ICO works in collaboration with various organisations, including governments, non-governmental organisations, and industry stakeholders, to amplify the impact of its initiatives. The partnerships aim to provide additional resources, expertise, and support to smallholder farmers in achieving sustainability. The ICO will need to be even more proactive in the development of collaborative partnerships in the various areas that its new agreement seeks particularly in addressing sustainability.

In 2022, the International Coffee Council concluded the negotiation of a new agreement that targets the emerging issues in the global industry, including the UN's Sustainable Development Goals (SDGs) as well as the role of the private sector and civil society. As at the publishing of this book, in 2023, ICO member governments were in the process of ratifying the new treaty. The ICO's mission is "to achieve sustainable expansion of the coffee sector in a market-based environment." It is hoped that under the implementation of the new International Coffee Agreement, ICA 2022, there will be some revolutionary changes for smallholder coffee farmers, aiming to improve their livelihoods, productivity, and resilience through the promotion of market transparency that should ensure real progress towards sustainability.

Inter-African Coffee Organisation Initiatives

The Inter-African Coffee Organisation (IACO) is one of the oldest pan-African inter-governmental organisations representing 25

producer countries, almost half the states on the continent. IACO is a platform for institutional cooperation enabling the sharing of information and networking.
More importantly, IACO acts as a bridge to solicit regional projects and technical assistance to strengthen capacities and facilitate support from other financial partners like the African Development Bank (AfDB) and African Export-Import Bank (Afreximbank).

The following initiatives and partnerships were undertaken for the IACO member states:

1. ***African Coffee Scientific Conference***: The African Coffee Scientific Conference is one of the Africa Coffee Research Network (ACRN) tools to facilitate the exchange and dissemination of scientific information between IACO member states.

2. ***The African Coffee Symposium***: The African Coffee Symposium (ACS) was launched in November 2013 to engage the private sector as part of the IACO Annual Meetings. The ACS has championed collaboration between policymakers, government and the coffee private sector.

3. ***The Drink African Coffee Build Africa (DACBA)***. The DACBA initiative was launched in May 2021 to promote domestic consumption in the member states through a multi-stakeholder approach targeting the universities, private sector associations (sports, youth groups) public offices (MDAs, Police) and retail outlets.

4. ***The African Youth Barista Championship***: The African Youth Barista Championship (AYBC) was launched in November

2022, targeting African youth to build a coffee-drinking culture and create jobs.

5. ***The Inter Africa Coffee Training Institute (IACTI)*** was established in Abidjan in November 2022 as a joint venture between IACO and Café Continent (a private company) to train and equip youth with skills in roasting, brewing, cupping and barista.

6. ***The G25 Africa Coffee Summit***: The G25 Africa Coffee Summit was held in May 2022 as a political platform for Heads of State from the G25 to advocate for coffee to be adopted as a strategic crop at the AU.

7. ***The Africa Coffee Week (ACW)*** was launched in September 2023 as a united platform of African stakeholders to collectively address the challenges facing the industry and explore opportunities for the transformation of the coffee value chain. IACO will partner with the main coffee private sector associations in Africa (AFCA & ACRAM) to host the week every year during the month of February in the G25 member states.

8. ***The African Coffee Facility (ACF)***: A proposal was submitted to Afreximbank for a facility of USD 950 million to which the bank pledged USD 500 million. The creation of an African Coffee Development Fund is aimed at financing projects that provide solutions to the myriad of challenges across the African coffee value chain. The ACF is expected to fund the development of new processing facilities at origin. This is expected to add value and create jobs for the youth.

IACO is fully committed to the transformation of the African coffee sector in partnership with the African Continental Free

Trade Area (AfCFTA) and has adopted a new coffee agreement which was in the process of ratification by the respective member states and was expected to be implemented in 2024.

World Coffee Producers Forum

The WCPF provides a voice for coffee producers, allowing them to raise their concerns and advocate for policies that promote their interests. Producers can discuss market access, price volatility, climate change, social sustainability, and other issues affecting their livelihoods. The forum promotes fair and sustainable trade. It is a platform for producers to engage with potential buyers and industry leaders, fostering direct relationships and facilitating market access. WCPF events have included workshops and training sessions. The Forum promotes connections that provide technical assistance to grow the skills and knowledge of coffee producers. The capacity-building initiatives improve farming techniques, post-harvest practices, quality control, and sustainability measures.

The WCPF will likely continue to provide opportunities for disruptive engagements that challenge the status quo in the global coffee arena, where the prosperity of producers must constantly be on the agenda. This writer came across a statement that one person once made on social media and stated that "I like to know the person that I'm dealing with and not just the 'seller'. It creates bonds of relationships." These are the kinds of relationships that will foster the long-term sustainability of the industry.

Global Coffee Platform Collaborations

The Global Coffee Platform (GCP) collaborates with various industry initiatives, certification bodies, research institutions, and sustainability-focused organisations to advance its goals. By fostering collaboration and knowledge exchange, the GCP champions a more sustainable and resilient coffee sector. The GCP is a platform for sharing knowledge, research, and best practices. It facilitates learning and capacity building by providing access to resources, tools, and training programmes that can benefit producers and other stakeholders. It works with governments, international organisations, and other stakeholders to shape policies and create an enabling environment for sustainable coffee. The GCP supports the development and implementation of sustainability standards, metrics, and verification systems, and upholds transparency, accountability, and credibility in sustainability claims and initiatives.

In collaborative networks, GCP also promotes sustainability of production through youth engagement and the value chain in producer countries, given that the average age of the coffee farmer is around 60 years. Mobilisation of the private sector for sustainability of the global coffee value chain have led to commitments from various companies. Using the GCP equivalence mechanisms, countries are in a position to develop national codes that meet international sustainability criteria. So far, Kenya has accomplished this, with some other countries following a similar process. GCP has a goal to achieve specific targets by 2030, in line with the UN's global goals of rolling out various tools.

Conclusion

There is need for a virtuous circle that will lead to farmer prosperity worldwide. There must be a shared responsibility between all the global coffee value chain players. There is urgent need for measures to ensure the sustainability of global coffee production, and in this, the producer is the critical starting point. It is important to bring on board roasters, retailers and distributors into a reporting mechanism that promotes transparency in the global value chain and strengthens the relationships between supply chain partners and clients. Promoting a circular communication loop that informs of the status of the producers will enhance accountability in dealing with poverty among producing communities, highlighting actions taken to address poverty. Initiatives that promote entrepreneurship, as well as leadership development, are needed to boost the capacity of the producing countries to proactively pursue the desired sustainability.

12

My Story

I was born to a father who was a coffee farmer in central Uganda. I do not recall my mother doing much about the coffee except supervising our different chores. We cultivated much coffee all around, and my father hired casual labourers to weed the farm. Family labour was involved in the harvesting, and I learned how to pick cherries off the tree. Initially, I did not know how to do it properly, so I just stripped the branch, taking off ripe and unripe cherries. It was the quick way to get the job done. I remember being reprimanded, albeit gently, and told that what I did was not good for the coffee tree. Much later, I learned why harvesting only the ripe cherries was essential. Later in life, I ended up in a coffee career, and worked both in the public and private sectors, locally and internationally, and got to understand the industry's intricacies more.

In the late 1980s, after completing my Master's degree and initially working at Daystar University in Nairobi, Kenya, I returned to Uganda and worked as a Planning Economist in the Ministry of Cooperatives and Marketing (my doctoral studies later focused on entrepreneurial leadership in the coffee industry in Africa). After a while, I was assigned to the team that worked on a World Bank project to restructure agricultural marketing in Uganda. As civil servants, some of us worked as counterparts to international consultants on this project. The restructuring of the Coffee Marketing Board was a big priority for the government because of the delays in payment to farmers due to inadequate crop finance to pay for all the coffee when delivered for export processing.

In 1991, I was seconded to serve in the Coffee Monitoring Unit (CMU) in the Agricultural Secretariat of the Bank of Uganda (the central bank) where I worked as the Coffee Budget Desk officer. The establishment of the CMU was integral to setting up the new industry regulatory agency known as the Uganda Coffee Development Authority (UCDA), of which I was one of the pioneers. Working in the UCDA was a very enriching professional experience as we developed systems to guide the liberalisation of the coffee industry in Uganda and developed data collection templates and reports still in use. In 1993, I was invited to join a team of African professionals working in the commodities sector, constituted by the International Trade Center (ITC) to engage in the preparation of training materials and writing case studies for training marketing managers in Africa. It was a rigorous exercise, and I was delighted that two of my cases were published in the ITC case book.

While at UCDA, I interacted with coffee processors and exporters and noted a significant knowledge gap and a need to professionalise the sector. After five years in the public sector, I joined the private sector where I helped set up the Uganda Coffee Trade Federation (UCTF) which later transformed into the Uganda Coffee Federation. At that time, there was great suspicion between UCDA and the coffee exporters, and I took up the challenge to work towards creating harmony in the industry.

I established the UCTF Secretariat and its services and sought to bring together the exporters to pursue a pre-competitive strategy that would work in their common interests. The secretariat coordinated policy dialogue, training, data collection and information sharing. I facilitated the consultative process of developing common positions by the exporters to present to the government, which helped the industry address various policy issues. I had a hand in developing the self-regulatory mechanisms that the private sector could use to ensure discipline within their ranks and an arbitration system for resolving disputes. UCTF's arbitration system was before Uganda had developed the general legal structure for alternative dispute resolution. UCTF also played a significant role in developing a warehouse receipt system in Uganda and worked with the World Bank in training exporters on risk management.

It was also critical to have training for the proprietors and staff of the coffee exporting companies to build capacity in running of their business. I sought technical assistance that enabled us to train in-country and abroad. The training included the then-famous London Coffee Course,where, with EU support, we had contingents of coffee people travel to London for study. The course was significant in introducing exporters to an understanding of the operations of the global coffee business. Visits to coffee buyers and the London Commodity Exchange augmented the theory sessions, helping the exporters to understand international coffee trading, price-setting mechanisms and different approaches to risk management. We also obtained support from the Commonwealth Fund for Technical Cooperation, which helped build the capacity of the UCTF Secretariat. UCTF pioneered private sector efforts in promoting Uganda coffee in the US and European markets, including conducting the first Internet-linked coffee tasting session by experts in Kampala and Washington DC in September 1996 of the same samples of coffee and comparing notes electronically. The Uganda and US press covered the event, providing positive vibes for Uganda coffee. This happened at the time when the first Coffee and Migratory Bird Conference was convened by the Smithsonian Society at the Washington Zoo, Washington DC, leading to the origins of the certification label of *Migratory Bird-friendly coffee*. I was also glad to have been a part of the landmark event.

My work with UCTF was in the mid-to-late 1990s, and I was in my 30s and full of energy. Unfortunately, there were a lot of misunderstandings and persistent suspicions between the government and the private sector, and I got caught in between the two parties. The coffee exporters I represented thought I was working in the government's interests, while government officials viewed me with suspicion of covering up for the 'sins' of the exporters. However, the UCTF experience prepared me well for greater leadership responsibilities in my career. Challenges notwithstanding, in general, Uganda's liberalisation of the coffee industry was noted by development partners and others to be exemplary, with frequent invitations to both UCDA and UCTF to share the country's experience in many African and global forums.

From 1995, I was part of the Uganda delegation to the meetings of the ICO as a representative of the private sector, and I was able to develop relationships with many coffee luminaries. The ICO

Executive Director invited me for consultative meetings between him and other private sector representatives seeking advice on how to create an appropriate role for the private sector in an inter-governmental entity such as the ICO. We proposed the creation of a Private Sector Committee, which the Executive Director presented to the Executive Board and the Council at the time and was adopted after much debate. It was to be considered in the text of the new treaty. The other contribution was a presentation requesting the Council to consider environmental sustainability to be embedded in the text of the new Agreement. This too was taken on board when the text of the new Agreement was debated. Through Resolution 393 of the ICC, the text of the Agreement was formally adopted on 27th September 2000, where the Private Sector Consultative Board (PSCB) was included as one of the organs of the ICO, and environmental sustainability was also taken on board in light of the UN Millennium Development Goals (MDGs). This was the sixth International Coffee Agreement (ICA), which entered into force provisionally on 1st October 2001 and definitively on 17th May 2005. I was proud to have been one of the contributors to the landmark changes in this important treaty.

UCTF recognised the significance of wild coffee in Uganda, taking note of the government's effort to protect the remaining wild coffee in the Kibale forest in western Uganda, gazetting it as a national park. UCTF worked closely with the Uganda Wildlife Authority (UWA) and Makerere University Institute of Environment and Natural Resources (MUIENR) to develop a community conservation project for communities around the Kibale National Park. MUIENR was established in 1988 in response to increasing concern by the government and the university about environmental degradation with a mandate to promote the development of knowledge, skills and positive attitudes for sustainable management of the ecosystem and natural resources through training and research. The university established a post, Makerere University Biological Field Station (MUBFS), within the national park to collect data and provide reports on various trends. Much research was undertaken on the wild crop. Given that Uganda is the epicentre of the origin of Robusta coffee, UCTF was proud to be associated with the efforts to conserve Uganda's wild varieties.

In 1999, I was appointed to serve as one of the members of the board of advisors for the International Task Force on Commodity Risk Management, whose secretariat was at the World Bank headquarters in Washington DC. We had several meetings in Africa, Europe and the USA in the quest to obtain information on the challenges faced by coffee producers, the practices and approaches in mitigating risks in international commodity trading, and how these could be adapted for use in low-income coffee-producing countries. This also led to my stint as a consultant coffee expert with the World Bank at the headquarters, where I joined a team that was developing the appropriate instruments for commodity risk management and identifying partners who could help in rolling out services in developing countries.

In some forums in East Africa between 1997 and 1998, discussions ensued on how others could benefit from the Uganda experience. I was tasked with designing a mechanism to help the African coffee private sector unite and pursue a common strategy in dealing with coffee buyers and importers. Commencing with consultations in 1999, I proposed the creation of the African Coffee Association. It was agreed that the organisation could start as an East African effort and later cover the rest of Africa. The consultations concluded in May 2000, with the resolution that I would take the lead in registering the new organisation known as the Eastern African Fine Coffees Association (EAFCA), which was later to become the African Fine Coffees Association (AFCA).

Thus, in 2000 I left UCTF to start EAFCA and set up its secretariat. I was 40 years old then and excited by the new challenge. With support from initial funding that I obtained from a US-AID project that focused on promoting sustainable tree crops in Africa, EAFCA took off on a sound footing. With the help of Dr. Jeff Hill, at USAID Washington, DC, we also obtained a USD 4 million grant from the American Government which was administered under a USAID project that covered Eastern and Southern Africa. I conceived a sustainability strategy to guarantee continuity after the end of grant funding, and in February 2004, I launched the African Fine Coffee Conference and Exhibition. The meeting was designed as an annual exposition hosted by a different country every year to allow coffee buyers to appreciate the diversity and variety of the different African coffees and to generate revenue to finance the association's operations. *(This was a great model that worked quite well until the disruptions of COVID-19 when, for two years, the exposition could not take place!)*

From 2004, I was part of the team that held a series of consultative meetings and workshops in developing the Common Code for the Coffee Community, also known as the 4Cs. Funding from the German and Swiss governments played was critical in supporting the consultations in developing the 4Cs, which evolved into the 4C Association as a membership organisation. Finally, it led to the creation of the Global Coffee Platform (GCP) as its successor in continuing to develop the Code and facilitating the global dialogue on coffee sustainability. At the time of writing this book, I am a member of the GCP and continue to play a role in influencing the global coffee sustainability agenda.

After establishing EAFCA, while I continued to serve as a board member, I handed over its leadership to a new team, set up my own coffee company, and concentrated on a consulting career. However, not too long after that, I was called upon by the government of Uganda to consider a nomination to run for the office of the Secretary General of the Inter-African Coffee Organisation (IACO), which I accepted after prayerful consideration. I was elected and subsequently took office as Secretary General in January 2013 at the IACO headquarters in Abidjan, Côte d'Ivoire. At IACO, we undertook several reforms in transforming the organisation and spearheading a new Agreement that would bring African coffee-producing and consuming countries under one entity. As an inter-governmental organisation, it did not have a private sector focus. Thus, during my term in office, we endeavoured to proactively engage the private sector and involve them in an annual coffee symposium (which we launched in November 2013), where they would actively discuss Africa's coffee policy agenda. Having retired from IACO and been nominated as a goodwill ambassador for African coffee by the IACO's 60th Annual General Assembly of 2020, I look back with gratitude to God for enabling me to contribute to the coffee industry at national, regional and international levels.

I am personally grateful to the government of Uganda for the opportunities I have had to develop my career in leadership in general and in the coffee industry in particular. As a young officer in the Ministry of Cooperatives and Marketing in the latter 1980s after my graduate studies, the Permanent Secretary, Mr Samuel B. Rutega, gave me a lot of responsibilities. I drafted many important statements and policy papers for both my Commissioner and Chief Planning Officer in the Ministry, and for the Permanent Secretary. I was given several assignments that challenged me and propelled me forward. Serving on the Working Group for the liberalisation of the coffee marketing system, the Coffee Monitoring Unit of the Bank of Uganda, and later being on the core team as pioneers of the Uganda Coffee Development Authority in the early to mid-1990s, was fundamental in my understanding of the workings of the industry locally and internationally.

I pay special tribute to all the colleagues that I have worked with through the years of my career in the industry, in the public and private sectors. I learnt a lot from Hon. Tress Bucyanayandi, the late Ambassador William Naggaga, Mr. Henry Ngabirano, and several others during my time at UCDA. I express gratitude to former colleagues at UCDA, including Dr Peter Ngategize, Nathan Uringi, the late James Serunjogi, Ambassador Solomon Rutega, Alice Gowa, David Kiwanuka, Julius Madira, Phoebe Kazinduki and several others. In establishing the Uganda Coffee Trade Federation and later the Eastern African Fine Coffees Association, I was greatly supported by efficient teams. I would like to particularly mention Hon. Robert Waggwa Nsibirwa, Ambassador Solomon Rutega, Mr John Byarugaba, Mrs Mary Kakooza-Kizza and Mrs Dorcas Mugarura, and thank them for their various contributions to the achievements that we made in this coffee journey. I am also grateful to different organisations and companies that committed to supporting our various efforts as partners, sponsors and exhibitors for their great contribution to the success of events such as the AFCA annual conference and exhibition.

The gentlemen who were extremely supportive as we started

EAFCA included Simeon Onchere, Paul Mugambwa, Hannington Karuhanga, and Hajj Ishak Lukenge, who deserve mention here. Dr Hill, from the Bureau for Africa in the US Department of Agriculture, was incredibly instrumental in getting the financial and technical assistance I needed to establish EAFCA and the annual conference that soon became self-sustaining. I am greatly indebted to him for his help in my journey of building that organisation. I also pay tribute to colleagues that I worked with at the World Bank, including Dr Nawal Kamel, Funke Oyewole, Dr Kangbin Zhang, Dr Ning Zhu, Lamon Rutten and others, partners in setting up the commodity risk management system which, among other things, was intended to help coffee farmers achieve sustainability through access to modern price risk-management instruments.

One key lesson I learnt throughout my career was that it was critical to build capacity and empower those I worked with, to ensure they could also advance in their respective careers. This is a key aspect of institutional sustainability. I am, therefore, proud to see that people who were part of my team have gone on to be very successful in their respective professional journeys. A significant preoccupation I have also had has been the need to address service delivery and the sustainability of the organisations I have led. One of my key leadership principles is respect for people. I honour all the staff in the organisation up to the lowest level, and I greet them courteously and listen to them when they have issues to express or ideas to contribute. I will say that in all the different leadership positions I have held, I know that the different team members from my work at UCDA to the different organisations I have led will express that they appreciated my compassionate and supportive leadership approach.

What I would consider the most significant achievement I had at AFCA is the annual conference and exhibition, which was my concept of how we could address the creation of opportunities for African coffee producers, processors and exporters to interact with international coffee buyers and roasters. I also envisioned this event as a significant contributor to the organisation's financial sustainability and, admittedly, it brings in the bulk of AFCA's revenue. The conference was to rotate in the different countries and provide opportunities for coffee safaris and discovery of the coffees of different African countries by our visitors. When I got the AFCA Lifetime Achievement Award at the AFCA conference in Kampala in February 2018, I was greatly delighted to receive it in the place where it all started. I was especially pleased when the AFCA Board of Directors remembered that I was a significant part of the start of the AFCA journey and for nominating me for that honour, a few years after it had been created.

I was the Secretary General of the Inter-African Coffee Organisation (IACO) when I received the Lifetime Achievement Award from AFCA. I was proud to carry the Uganda flag and share the Uganda coffee experience. I am grateful to my staff at IACO, with whom we worked diligently to put African coffee on a new pedestal and to raise the profile of our pan-African organisation, including the finalisation of the new IACO Agreement that was still in the process of ratification by the member statesby the time of writing. When I took charge at IACO, it was an organisation of only coffee-producing countries. However, the new treaty, bringing together all African-producing and consuming countries, clearly articulates the role of the private sector and aims to take full advantage of the African Continental Free Trade Area (AfCFTA). I am grateful to the former Prime Minister of Ethiopia, His Excellency Hailemariam Desalegn, who accepted the request to serve as the IACO Patron and has done a phenomenal job of promoting the cause of African coffees. I also express gratitude to Dr. Donald Kaberuka, former President of the African Development Bank, and Prof. Benedict Oramah, President of Afreximbank, for their roles in putting coffee high on the agendas of their respective institutions. Dr Denis Seudieu, who I first met in the mid-1990s, when he joined the ICO as Chief Economist, has been a great friend with whom we have walked the coffee journey. I am so grateful for all the support that I received from him over more than two decades.

I further express gratitude to my predecessor as IACO Secretary General and presently Commissioner for Agriculture, Rural Development, Blue Economy and Sustainable Environment at the African Union Commission, Ambassador Josefa Sacko, for her relentless support in the effort to put coffee on the strategic agenda of the African Union. I also do salute colleagues at CABI Africa Regional Office, particularly Dr Morris Akiri and Dr Charles Agwanda, for their tremendous support to the cause of the African coffee industry and who, together with Mrs Nancy Cheruiyot, the CEO of the Commodity Fund-Kenya, provided excellent support in IACO's launch of the partnership development for the Africa Coffee Facility. We still have a long way to go, but we appreciate support and goodwill from individuals such as Dr Leonard Mizzi, the Head of the Unit for International Partnerships - Sustainable Agri-Food Systems and Fisheries at the European Commission, Directorate-General (DG). I am also very grateful for the hospitality of the Government of Cote d'Ivoire during my stay in Abidjan, and also express gratitude to the various communities and fellowships in Abidjan where I was well received and enjoyed a great time during my stay, becoming a home away from home.

Given my engagement with the World Coffee Producers Forum, I would like acknowledge different colleagues with whom we have worked together led by the team from the Colombian Coffee Federation, the Brazilian Specialty Coffee Association, the India Coffee Trust, the African Fine Coffees Association and the Agency for Robusta in Africa and Madagascar. While I cannot be exhaustive, special mention is made of Dr Roberto Velez, Dr Juan Esteban Orduz, Dr Vanusia Nogueira, Madhu Boponna, Dr Enselme Gouthon, Michael Ndoping, Omer Gratien Maledy, Dr Emmanuel Iyamulemye and Dr Adugna Debele.

I express gratitude to the Government of Uganda for their confidence in me to nominate me for the role of Secretary General of IACO, where I served diligently for two full terms. My passion as Africa's Coffee Ambassador is to see the transformation of the value chain on the continent and the elimination of poverty among coffee-producing communities. We have much work to do in the professionalisation of the industry. African coffee farmers must graduate from subsistence agriculture to a more modern approach, adopting good agronomic and agricultural practices and regenerative approaches that promote environmental conservation. Worldwide, biodiversity conservation efforts are helping promote better environmental stewardship, though some of these efforts are few and far between and must essentially be scaled up in many African countries.

Finally, I thank my beloved wife, Miriam, who has been a faithful partner all throughout this journey and without whom I would not have attained this that I celebrate today. I also thank my children Olivia, Katalina and Enoka, who have been great cheerleaders. Most significantly, I thank the Almighty God and give Him all the glory, honour and praise, because it is in Him that I live and move and have my being.

Useful Reference Resources

The **International Trade Centre** (ITC) provides useful information on coffee. It supports the global coffee sector to evolve efficient supply chains from seed to cup for the benefit of all actors. The Coffee Exporters' Guide is a useful reference resource made available by ITC to benefit coffee exporters worldwide.

With respect to health-related information, there are also several reputable websites with studies and research on the health benefits of drinking coffee. Below are some reliable sources to explore:

National Institutes of Health (NIH) - PubMed: PubMed is a comprehensive database of scientific articles, including many studies on the health effects of coffee. It provides access to research papers from various medical and scientific journals. To find relevant studies, one can search for specific topics or or use keywords.

The American Heart Association (AHA): The AHA website provides cardiovascular health information, often covering coffee consumption and heart health research. One can explore the AHA website for articles and research summaries discussing coffee consumption's potential benefits or risks.

Harvard T.H. Chan School of Public Health: The Harvard School of Public Health frequently publishes research and articles on various health topics, including coffee and its effects on health. Their website provides valuable information based on scientific studies and can be a helpful resource for understanding the latest research findings.

Mayo Clinic: Mayo Clinic is a renowned medical institution that offers reliable health information to the public. Their website covers many topics, including coffee and its potential health benefits. They provide summaries of research studies and expert insights.

The National Coffee Association (NCA): The NCA is an industry association that represents coffee companies and professionals. Their website often features research summaries, news articles, and reports on coffee and health. While the NCA represents the coffee industry, they typically rely on scientific studies and reputable sources in their publications.

It is worth noting that while these websites provide valuable information, it is crucial to critically evaluate the studies and consider the overall body of evidence. Individual studies may present specific findings, but the scientific consensus is typically based on a comprehensive analysis of multiple studies. Consulting with healthcare professionals or registered dietitians can also provide personalised guidance based on one's specific health needs and circumstances.

There are also several reputable websites in Europe to find studies and research on the health benefits of drinking coffee. Some of the reliable sources that one can further explore include the following:

European Food Safety Authority (EFSA): EFSA is an agency of the European Union responsible for providing scientific advice and communication on food and beverages. Their website contains scientific opinions and assessments related to various food and beverage topics, including coffee. One can search their database for specific evaluations and reports on the health effects of coffee.

European Society of Cardiology (ESC): The ESC is a professional association dedicated to cardiovascular health. The ESC website features news articles, research summaries, heart health guidelines, and coffee consumption studies. One can find valuable insights on the cardiovascular effects of coffee from a European perspective.

European Journal of Clinical Nutrition (EJCN): The EJCN is a peer-reviewed scientific journal that publishes research related to clinical nutrition. Their website provides access to published articles, including studies on the health effects of coffee. One can search their database or browse through their issues to find relevant research papers.

Please note that these websites may feature studies and research conducted in Europe or globally. It is essential to evaluate the studies critically, consider the overall body of evidence, and consult with healthcare professionals for personalised guidance.

Apart from the US and Europe, there are several reputable websites in Asia where one can find studies and research on the health benefits of drinking coffee. Here are some reliable sources one can explore:

National Center for Biotechnology Information (NCBI): The NCBI is a U.S. National Library of Medicine resource that provides access to a vast collection of scientific articles and studies. It includes research from around the world, including Asia. One can search for coffee-related studies using their PubMed database, which covers a wide range of health-related topics.

Asia Pacific Journal of Clinical Nutrition (APJCN): APJCN is a peer-reviewed journal that focuses on clinical nutrition research in the Asia-Pacific region. Their website provides access to published articles, including studies on the health effects of coffee. One can explore their database or browse through their issues to find relevant research papers.

The Japan Coffee Association: The Japan Coffee Association is an organisation dedicated to promoting coffee consumption and research in Japan. Their website often features articles and research summaries related to coffee and health. They provide information on scientific studies conducted in Japan and beyond.

Korean Society of Food Science and Technology (KoSFoST): KoSFoST is a professional society in South Korea that focuses on food science and technology. Their website includes publications, research articles, and conference proceedings related to various aspects of food, including coffee and its health effects. One can find valuable insights from Korean researchers and scientists.

These websites can serve as valuable resources for finding studies conducted in Asia and accessing research on the health benefits of drinking coffee. However, it is essential to critically evaluate the studies and consider the overall body of evidence. Consulting with healthcare professionals or registered dietitians can also provide personalised guidance based on one's specific health needs and circumstances.

Other Useful References Resources

Choi, H.K., Willett, W. and Curhan, G. (2007), Coffee consumption and risk of incident gout in men: A prospective study. Arthritis & Rheumatism, 56: 2049-2055. https://doi.org/10.1002/art.22712

Kalema-Zikusoka, G. (2023). Walking with gorillas: the journey of an African wildlife vet. Arcade Publishing, NY, New York.

https://en.avpa.fr/cafes

https://intelligence.coffee/2023/03/direct-trade-coffee-associations/

https://www.standup4humanrights.org/layout/files/30on30/UDHR70-30on30-article25-eng.pdf

https://worldpopulationreview.com/country-rankings/coffee-consumption-by-country

https://www.un.org/en/about-us/universal-declaration-of-human-rights

https://wfto.com/about-us/history-wfto/history-fair-trade#

https://corporatefinanceinstitute.com/resources/commodities/new-york-board-of-trade-nybot/

https://corporatefinanceinstitute.com/resources/derivatives/london-international-financial-futures-exchange-liffe/

https://www.un.org/en/about-us/universal-declaration-of-human-rights

https://ophi.org.uk/multidimensional-poverty-index/

https://hdr.undp.org/publication/citation-export/3389

https://ico.org/

https://www.mordorintelligence.com/industry-reports/europe-coffee-market

https://www.statista.com/topics/4023/coffee-market-in-europe/

https://www.market-inspector.co.uk/blog/2019/04/coffee-culture-western-europe

https://landgeist.com/2022/04/19/coffee-consumption-in-europe/

https://fullcoffeeroast.com/best-european-coffee-brands/

https://fullcoffeeroast.com/how-many-people-in-the-world-drink-coffee/

https://www.worldatlas.com/articles/top-10-coffee-consuming-nations.html

https://worldpopulationreview.com/country-rankings/coffee-consumption-by-country

https://hdr.undp.org/content/2022-global-multidimensional-poverty-index-mpi#/indicies/MPI

https://health.clevelandclinic.org/the-health-benefits-of-coffee/

www.cbi.eu/market-information/coffee/trade-statistics

https://www.hopkinsmedicine.org/health/wellness-and-prevention/9-reasons-why-the-right-amount-of-coffee-is-good-for-you

https://dailycoffeenews.com/2023/05/11/frances-avpa-holding-9th-coffees-roasted-at-origin-competition/

https://www.mordorintelligence.com/industry-reports/china-coffee-market

https://coffeeaffection.com/china-coffee-consumption-statistics/

https://worldcoffeeresearch.org/focus-countries/

https://www.statista.com/topics/6546/coffee-market-in-indonesia/

https://en.wikipedia.org/wiki/Coffee_production_in_Indonesia

https://www.statista.com/statistics/706965/production-of-coffee-in-indonesia/.

https://www.fas.usda.gov/data/

https://en.wikipedia.org/wiki/Coffee_production_in_Honduras.

https://coffeehunter.com/our-origins/honduras/.

https://www.ibef.org/exports/coffee-industry-in-india

https://www.statista.com/statistics/1048925/india-coffee-total-production-volume/

https://en.wikipedia.org/wiki/Coffee_production_in_India

https://www.statista.com/topics/4590/coffee-market-in-india/

Pendergrast, M. (2010). Uncommon grounds: *The history of coffee and how it transformed our world. Basic Books.*

About the Author

FRED KAWUMA, the African Coffee Ambassador, is Secretary-General Emeritus of the Inter-African Coffee Organisation (IACO), and one of the founders of the World Coffee Producers Forum. He founded the African Fine Coffees Association and was its first Executive Director. He was also the founder of the Uganda Coffee Federation and one of the pioneers of the Uganda Coffee Development Authority. Fred conceptualised the African Fine Coffee Conference and Exhibition as an opportunity to link African producers and exporters with buyers and roasters globally, which he launched in Feb 2004. He is an experienced executive, consultant, coffee professional, and champion of coffee improvement systems from production through the value chain to the consumer. He has worked as a coffee expert in the public and private sectors in Africa and the United States. Currently, he is the Chairman of Café Africa Uganda. He also serves on several local and international boards. He has been a CEO in different organisations. He has received awards for his work in coffee—a commendation from the US Congress in 2004, an Award of Coffee Excellence from the President of Uganda in 2017 as one of the pioneers of UCDA, and the AFCA Lifetime Achievement Award in 2018. He was appointed Goodwill Ambassador for African Coffee in November 2020. Fred holds a Bachelor of Commerce (Hons) in Marketing from Makerere University, an MA in Communication from Wheaton College, IL, USA, and a PhD in Entrepreneurial Leadership from Regent University, VA, USA.

He can be reached at P.O. Box 10974, Kampala, Uganada, *fkawuma@gmail.com*, *fredkaw@mail.regent.edu* or *info@fredkawuma.com* Tel: +256 776 700190

www.ingramcontent.com/pod-product-compliance
Lightning Source LLC
LaVergne TN
LVHW052006160826
845678LV00005B/1663

* 9 7 8 9 9 1 3 9 7 4 3 0 1 *